LOVE
ONE
ANOTHER

Stories Families Love To Retell

REV. LUCIUS CERVANTES

LOVE ONE ANOTHER

STORIES FAMILIES LOVE TO RETELL

Kravitz & Sons
INNOVATORS IN PUBLISHING, MARKETING AND ADVERTISING

Kravitz and Sons LLC
1301 Farmville Blvd, Suite 104
Greenville, NC 27834

Published by Kravitz and Sons LLC.

ISBN: 979-8-89639-214-9 (sc)
ISBN: 979-8-89639-215-6 (e)

Library of Congress Control Number: 979-8-89639-214-9

TABLE OF CONTENTS

To
Mayor Alfonso and Carmen Davis Cervantes
Richard and Mary Casey
Anthony and Mary Anne Sansone Sr.

Foreword

How Do I Love Thee?

This is a collection of more than two hundred stories. It is a book written by a Jesuit Sociology Professor, Father Lu Cervantes. I ran across both him and his short stories when I was making the Exercises of St. Ignatius at Jesuit Hall on the campus of St. Louis University. I converted to Catholicism.

During the past year, the better half of myself, Joan Klump Mitchell, died and left me bereft. During this period I have had time to think over more carefully what life is all about.

My wife, Joan, and I for years appreciated the company of Father Lu and his stories, which are basically included in this volume. We came to believe that others besides those parishioners at Saint Mathias Church, where Father Lu is a celebrant every Sunday, and the men with our Manresa Study Club would profit reading these stories.

This Christmas I decided to take this selection of the Cervantes short stories and make them a gift to you. They were originally called A Thought for Today. Joan and I enjoyed them all throughout our married life.

Father Lu Cervantes was the witness priest at our nuptial mass when we became one. Through our marriage and at Joan's "We Love YOU" surprise party when she first discovered she had cancer, and again at her funeral mass, Lu's words were always with us. On this occasion and on others, Joan and I were moved by his eloquent rendition of Elizabeth Barrett Browning's sonnet to her husband, "How Do I Love Thee?" It is Father Lu's signature poem.

How Do I Love Thee?

How do I love thee? Let me count the ways.
I love thee to the depth and breadth and height
My soul can reach, when feeling out of sight
For the ends of Being and ideal Grace.
I love thee to the level of every day's
Most quiet need, by sun and candle light.
I love thee freely, as man strives for Right;
I love thee purely, as they turn from Praise.
I love thee with the passion put to use
In my old griefs, and with my childhood's faith.
I love thee with a love I seemed to lose
With my lost saints—I love thee with the breath
Smiles, tears, of all my life! —and, if God choose
I shall but love thee better after death.

In Joan's beautiful serene death without quivering or gurgling but only a slight smile, a glow to her complexion and open hands, with her head turned to the window looking out at the bright afternoon light, the words of Robert Browning, Poet Laureate of England, to his dying wife, came to my mind:

Grow old along with me.
The best is yet to be

The last of life for which the first was made.
Our times are in his hand
Who saith, "A whole I planned;
Youth shows but half; trust God: see all,
Nor be afraid."

May the gift of Father Lu Cervantes and Joan's Love and guidance to me be this Gift of love to you.

—Melvin W. Mitchell
LTC, USA

THE BRIDGE OF LIFE

The famous novelist Thornton Wilder opens his work *The Bridge of San Luis Rey* with a brief account of the collapse of a bridge, hurling to sudden destruction a little group of people crossing it. Then Wilder goes back and sketches the life of each of the victims, searching for some clue to solve the riddle of why these particular individuals should have had their lives snuffed out so suddenly and with such apparently blind indiscrimination.

He ends his inquiry by pointing to the only factor he has been able to find, which gives meaning to life and constitutes the bridge of life to those who are gone. It is in the final sentence and the no-blest line in the whole novel: "There is a land of the living and a land of the dead and the bridge is love, the only survival, the only meaning.

Friends, "It is love and love alone the world is seeking; it is love and love alone that rules the world."

"Grow Old Along with Me"

There is something very beautiful about a couple who have grown old together. President Harry Truman and his wife Bess: or Presi-dent Ronald Reagan and his wife Nancy: so likewise President George Bush and his wife Barbara showed forth the nubile clarity of the phrase "Grow old along with me." Whether or not the younger President George W. Bush and his wife Laura (much less former President William Jefferson Clinton and his wife Senator Hillary Rodham Clinton) will qualify as American icons of "till death do us part" has yet to be revealed.

In the movie *On Golden Pond*, Katherine Hepburn and Henry Fonda showed us what an ideal elderly couple would look like. Scripture tells us that a brother helped by a brother is like a strong city. Even more so is that true of a loving husband and wife.

Perhaps the most famous of all elderly couples is Robert and Elizabeth Barrett Browning. As Colonel Melvin Mitchell pointed out in the Foreword, Robert Browning was the Poet Laureate of England and his wife Elizabeth authored the volume *Sonnets of the Portuguese*.

In this latter collection, we find what is arguably the most beautiful sonnet in the English language: "How Do I Love Thee?" It was to this famous question that Robert replied lyrically, "Grow old along with me. . . ." Both of these classic poems are found in the text of the Foreword by Melvin Mitchell.

"Repetition is the mother of studies," states the old Latin proverb. That truism is just as true in the present instance of Robert Browning's reply to his wife:

Grow old along with me.
The best is yet to be
The last of life for which the first was made.
Our times are in his hand
Who saith, "A whole I planned;
Youth shows but half; trust God: see all,
Nor be afraid."

A Hospital Scene

It was in the Colorado General Hospital. A young father of a large family lay dying. The relatives, children, the nurse, the doctor, and I, the priest, now stepped out of the room into the corridor so that the distraught young wife might be alone with the husband whom she would see no more on this earth.

After a few minutes, as we were standing there in that quiet, darkened hallway, we saw the shadow of the young mother who was soon to be a widow, emerging from the door of that room of death. Suddenly the shadow stopped, wheeled around, and we could not help but hear those last poignant burning words: "Darling, I love you." And from the depths of that hospital room and from the deeper depths of that dying husband, echoed the glorious triumphant cry of his kindred soul: "And, darling, I love you."

"It is love and love alone the world is seeking; it is love and love alone that rules the world." Each of us is seeking love. God is love. "Our hearts were made for Thee," O God, and they will not rest until they find their rest in Thee.

THE EVIL WITCH AND
THE BEAUTIFUL RAPUNZEL

Do you remember the folktale, that children's fairy tale story of the wicked witch and the beautiful Rapunzel? The story begins with "Once upon a time" and ends with "and they lived happily ever after."

But in between many wonderful incidents happened. The evil witch had imprisoned Rapunzel in a high tower in the dark woods, dressed her in rags, fed her crusts of bread, and despite the fact that Rapunzel was very beautiful, the witch always told her she was plain and dull and ugly. And Rapunzel believed her. For how else would she know? It wasn't until the handsome prince came to slay the evil witch and free Rapunzel, that Rapunzel saw in the eyes of the handsome prince how beautiful and wonderful she really was.

In a way the story of Rapunzel is a story of us all. We do not realize how wonderful and handsomely beautiful we really are, how we are made to the image and likeness of God himself, until we see that fact mirrored in the eyes of Jesus Christ, the real prince charming and Son of God.

The Peasant Woman and Her Onion

The famous Russian novelist Dostoevsky tells the story about an evil peasant woman who had done only one good thing in all her life she had given an onion to a beggar woman. When she died, the devils threw her into a lake of fire. But God told the evil woman's guardian angel to take that onion, hold it out to her in the lake, and let her take hold to be pulled out. The angel flew to the evil woman in the burning lake, held out the onion to her, and said: "Catch hold of this onion, and I'll try to pull you out." And he began cautiously pulling her out. He had just raised her halfway out, when the other sinners in the lake, seeing how she was being drawn out, began to catch hold of her so as to be pulled out with her.

But she was a very wicked woman and began kicking them: "I'm the one to be pulled out, not you. It's my onion, not yours." As soon as she said that, the onion broke. The woman fell back into the lake, and she is burning there to this day. So the angel wept and went away.

God Loves You

There was a true story in the *Reader's Digest* of a homely and lonely little orphan girl. She wasn't liked. She didn't mix. She couldn't do anything. She didn't have one real friend.

One day the authorities saw her going down to the highway; they saw her attaching a note to one of the lower branches. When these authorities later obtained that note, here is what it said: "Whoever sees this, I want you to know 'I love you.' "

That poor little girl is typical of all of us; we dreadfully, distressingly, want someone to love us individually. The same psychological fact holds in our relationship with God. We long to love God and be loved as an individual in return. But God *does* love each of us even as though there were only one of us. There were a million other individuals God could have made instead of you, but he chose you. God says, "I have loved you with an everlasting love; therefore I have drawn you out of nothing."

Look at your crucifix. It likewise contains the message hung on the tree of the cross, and as the little orphan girl's message, it reads: "Whoever sees this, I want you to know I love you."

Science Looks to Love

World-famous scientist Harvard Professor Pitirim A. Sorokin had this to say about love: "From the tragic experience of the last few decades, we scientists have begun to learn that, without a minimum of love, no social harmony, no peace of mind, no freedom and no happiness are possible.

"Love is a life-giving force, loving persons live longer," says Sorokin, "love annuls loneliness and is the best antidote to suicidal tendencies: love is freedom at its loftiest; love is fearless and is the best remedy for any fear, love is the most creative power; love is the accessible and effective means to peace of mind and supreme happiness; love is the best therapy against hate, insanity, misery, death and destruction; finally, love is the only means of transcending the narrow limits of our Lilliputian egos and of making our true self coextensive with God."

Do Unto Others

Here are two stories of self-interest:

A customer at a filling station was much impressed as he watched the meticulous care that an attendant was devoting to a nearby car.

"Now there's a real worker!" remarked the customer, to the manager of the station.

"Oh," replied the manager, "that's his own car!"

A husband said to his wife soon after they sat down in a movie, "Can you see okay? Is there any draft? Is there anyone with a toe of a shoe in the rear of the seat? Is there a woman in front of you with a big hat on? No? Would you mind changing seats with me?"

Friends: imagine a filling-station attendant being as interested in your car as he is in his own. Or imagine being as sensitive to the interests and convenience of your wife as that husband was to his own sensitivities about the draft, and toe of the shoe in the back of the seat, and the obstructing of his vision by the woman with the big hat seated in front of him at the movie.

But that is the kind of interest and love for others that our Lord challenges you to when he says: Do unto others as you would have done unto yourself.

Blindfolded Eyes and Straightened Elbows

The Fox Theatre is right around the corner from where I am now seated. There is the story of a little girl leading her tiny brother into the Fox Theatre and his eyes were blindfolded. The usher who was taking the tickets asked her: "Hey, little girl, is your tiny brother blind?" "No," the little girl responded. "He's not blind. I always bandage his eyes on the way to the movie, so when we get inside and it's all dark-then he can see and he leads me to the seats."

And there is the story of the theologian who went to hell just to see how things were. He found that everybody in hell had his or her arms in a plaster cast so that they couldn't bend their arms and feed themselves. In their frustration they were hitting each other with their knives and forks in a hateful way.

The theologian then went to heaven and found almost the same situation. Everyone had plaster casts on his or her arms so they couldn't bend their elbows, but rather than trying to feed themselves, they fed the person next to them.

The only difference between heaven and hell was that in hell there was no cooperation with one another; in heaven there was complete cooperation.

A Personal Quiz Program

Quiz programs are as old as the human race. Try this one. "Who is it who under all circumstances, in sickness and in health, in summer and in winter, at work and in play who is always seeking your greater convenience? Who is it who is so infatuated with you, so blind to your defects and sins that you never do a thing for which this person has not some kind of excuse or specious argument?"

There is only one person who will fit an answer to that quiz; it's not your best friend, it's not your mother or father, and it's not God. The only person who is blind to all your defects, who is constantly seeking your pleasure, is yourself.

Consider then the tremendous impact in your life, if you would follow Christ's injunction, "Love your neighbor as yourself." Think what it would mean in your life if you would really seek the joy and ease and comfort of others as you seek it for yourself. What a different world of love your world would be. That is the first step of love, which Christ bids you: love your neighbor as yourself.

Love in the Marketplace

Let me give you one example of how one man according to his lights put love of God and his fellowman into his daily economic life. His name was Henry Ford. Henry Ford was being sued by his stockholders because they believed that he was paying too high wages to the working men and charging too low prices to the public for the revolutionary Ford cars. He was being sued for putting the public before profit.

When Henry Ford was brought into court, he proclaimed, "I believe that business and industry are primarily a public service. 1 have had two goals in life: (1) To enable a large number of people to buy and enjoy the use of a car, and (2) to give a large number of men employment at good wages."

Henry Ford continued by saying, "I do not believe we should make such an awful profit on our cars. A reasonable profit is right, but not too much. So it has been my policy to force the price of the car down as fast as production would permit and give the benefits to users and laborers."

Friends, I call this *Love in the Marketplace.*

Actions Speak Louder Than Words

Actions speak louder than words. This phrase, actions speak louder than words, is especially true when it comes to love... in all love, there should be words. . . but not only words. Actions speak louder than words.

There was once upon a time a poetic youth who wrote his loved one a love letter that went like this: "My darling, I'd climb the highest mountain if I knew that when I'd climbed that highest mountain there I would find you; I'd walk across the hottest desert, if when I'd have crossed the hottest desert there I would find you; I'd swim the deepest ocean if when I'd swim that ocean, I knew that there I'd find you. All my love, (Signed) Egbert."

(And he added this postscript): "P.S. I'll be over tonight. . . if it doesn't rain."

Actions speak louder than words. And so with our love of God. Anyone who says he loves God and with his actions shows that he hates his brother. . . "is a liar". . . so states St. John the Evangelist. Actions speak louder than words.

"I Am Thyself"

There is the remarkable story frequently found in Arabian literature. The lover knocks at the door of the beloved and a voice asks from within: "Who art. Thou?" "I am Kahlil," he said. And the voice replied: "There is no room for thee and me in this house." And the door remained shut.

Then the lover retired to the desert and fasted and prayed in solitude. After a year he came back and knocked again at the door. Once again the voice asked: "Who art Thou?" "I am your brother," he answered. And the voice replied: "There is no room for both thee and me in this house." And the door remained shut.

9

After another year of fasting and prayer in the desert, the lover returned and one again knocked at the door. Once more the voice asked, "Who art thou?" He replied: "I am Thyself." And the door opened to him.

Friends, today say to the world that you come in contact with: "I am thyself." You'll be surprised how many doors will open to you.

Till Death Do Us Part

Yesterday I had a wedding. As a tribute to all brides and grooms, would you like to go over the ceremony with me? Here they stood, bride and groom, before this flower-laden and candle-lit altar. Like the altar, they seemed pure, strong, dedicated, and handsomely beautiful. Their two voices, as symbolic spokesmen for the millions of the world's lovers, now spoke those immortal words of undying love:

"I, Joseph, take thee, Mary, as my lawful wife, to have and to hold, from this day forward, for better, for worse, for richer, for poorer, in sickness and in health, until death do us part." And the bride's softer reply of soul to soul: "I, Mary, take thee, Joseph, as my lawful husband, to have and to hold, from this day forward, for better, for worse, for richer, for poorer, in sickness and in health, until death do us part."

And the blessing: "I join you together in marriage in the Name of the Father and the Son and the Holy Spirit."

Parenting

One day Michelangelo, the world's famous artist, was strolling through a back street of Florence with a friend. He stopped to examine a block of rough marble buried under dirt and rubbish. When his companion asked him what he wanted with that chunk of dirty rough rock, he gave his famous answer: "Oh, there's an angel in that stone, and I must let it out." After he had the block of rough marble carefully taken to his home, he set to work. By patient toil with chisel and mallet, he succeeded—he "brought the angel out."

What to others was an ordinary, shapeless, rough, unpolished mass of stone, was to the master's eye a hidden glory and a challenging possibility. He had to "bring the angel out."

And here is the glory of parenting. To take the rough marble of infant human nature that is half-buried under the clay and earthy down-drag of this world and, as Michelangelo, within one's home by patient toil with the chisel of discipline and the mallet of love to "bring the angel out." There is no greater career than parenting.

A Cave Man and His Son

A million years ago, a little boy turned his bright trusting eyes to his caveman father and asked: "Daddy, why is the sky blue?" The little boy thought sure his father would know the answer because fathers are giants and they're supposed to know everything. But Papa caveman didn't. He just told the child to go away.

A thousand generations of new children have trod the earth since that first disillusioned caveboy. A thousand generations of new children have asked their penetrating questions and listened to their parents' answers so they could form their own lives.

"Daddy, do fish close their eyes and sleep under water?"

"Daddy, where did I come from?" "Did the stork really bring me?" Knowledgeable and straightforward answers are in order. Depending upon the child's age and maturity, the basic facts are simple and beautiful: "Son that's how God made it. Here are the facts," and so forth.

You "Daddies," I suggest that you have some work to do to find out the answers to the questions that your childrens' queries pose to you. If you do learn answers for your children, the millennium will have arrived. Otherwise you are right back to the state of our caveman father and his illiterate offspring.

My Father

My father was an alcoholic. And that is why I can give you first-hand information as to what alcoholism can do to a wonderful individual, a highly successful businessman, married to an incredibly talented and beautiful woman, father of seven children, and in the early days, one of the most popular men in the City of St. Louis.

First of all, it ruined his career. And where there is Punch, there is Judy. His family life was ruined. There are no pictures of Dad in the family album after my younger brother, who became the Mayor of St. Louis, was three years old. Because Dad was gone. He lived to be seventy but an outcast of society. And, oh, what a glorious family life we could have had if Dad had not been an alcoholic. Thank God for Alcoholics Anonymous. AA will work for you if you will work with it. All of us can profit from the AA prayer:

God grant me the serenity to accept things I cannot change, courage to change things I can, and wisdom to know the difference.

My Mother

To Get a Friend—Be a Friend

I can remember the incident as if it were yesterday. My mother was eighty-four years old. My brother, former St. Louis Mayor A.J. Cervantes, and I were bringing our eighty-four-year-old mother to a nursing home. It was a trial run. We wanted to find out whether the home would have Mother and whether Mother would have the home. We nervously brought Mother to the retirement home, introduced her, and left her there by herself for an hour. Then we went back to pick her up to return her to her apartment where she had been living alone for so many years.

When we went back and to get her, thank God, Mother's face was bright and glowing and smiling. She liked it there at the nursing home. The wonderful people at St. Agnes had made Mother feel wanted. They needed her, they said. They needed her for others, because she was so friendly. And I am sure that the staff and residents at St. Agnes did need her and want her. She was alert and friendly and interested in others. And such is my theme today: All people especially the elderly can feel wanted by doing things that make them wanted. To get a friend-be a friend.

Obedience in Marriage?

Yesterday my nephew and namesake, Lucius Craig Cervantes, married Eileen Minor. At the wedding rehearsal the night before, we went over the marriage formula. First, Lucius recited the formula, and then Eileen repeated: "I, Eileen, take you, Lucius, for my lawful husband, to have and to hold, from this day forward, for better, for worse, for richer, for poorer, in sickness and in health, until death do us part."

And my nephew interrupted saying: "Hey, wait a minute. There's nothing there about *obedience*! Has the Church changed or what?" And all the wedding party laughed and thought it was funny. But they did look back over the formula (. . . "I take you as my lawful husband to have and to hold.". . .) and they all did wonder too... why isn't there anything about obedience? And the brief answer is: yes, the Church and society have both changed. The fidelity and love of the husband and wife are now stressed: "As Christ is to the Church."

Overpopulation and mass production bring women as well as men into the market place. Rather than through obedience, it is now on mutual love and fidelity that the relationship between husband and wife must depend.

Clean Hands

This true story happened in St. Mary's Hospital. As a Chaplain, I happened to be present with this very manly husband at the bedside of his wife. The nurse brought the squalling mite of a newborn child for the first-time look by the father. With the nurses' encouragement, he awkwardly took that baby into his strong hands. He paused unbelievingly for a moment and then took a step over to his smiling wife's bedside.

He looked at her, his eyes raised to heaven, and he solemnly said: "Dear God, I give You thanks that with our cooperation and through my wife, I have begotten a child." Then he took me aside and quietly explained to me: "Father, do you see these hands? Years ago I did not know whether to become a priest or a married man. But right then and there, I decided that whether I became a priest or a married man, I would bring these hands pure and clean either to God at the altar or to my wife in my home. And though at times the going was rough, God's grace was sufficient for me."

This proud young father made me appreciate the beauty and strength of purity as I had never realized it before.

Divorce

You will appreciate this letter. This was a woman who had no religious affiliation.

"Although happily married to a good Catholic," she writes, "I never gave any serious thought to religion until one afternoon my twelve-year-old daughter burst into the house and without preliminaries blurted out: "Mom, please become a Catholic, and then you'll never divorce Daddy."

"My first impulse was to laugh, but her serious expression told me there was a good reason for her impetuous plea. Drawing her close to me, I asked, 'Why do you say that, Sheila?'

" 'Well,' she replied, 'today Heather Thompson was crying because her father and mother have just been divorced. I told her not to worry. She said, 'You don't know how lucky you are, Sheila, your mommy and daddy will always be together because they're Catholics."

" 'I didn't tell her that you are not a Catholic, Mommy, but the awfulest feeling came over me that if you got real angry with Daddy sometime, you might divorce him.' "

"I held my daughter closer, and in a flash, I realized for the first time the love and protection that the Catholic Church throws about her children.

"Taking Sheila with me, I went straight to the parish priest and arranged for instructions."

Chastity

The gaunt hill of Calvary, just outside the walls of the City of Jerusalem, is the holiest land on earth. It was there that Christ suffered and died for all of us. Had you come to Calvary, a traveler or pilgrim, a hundred years after the death of Christ, you would have found a temple dedicated not to the suffering Christ, but to Incarnate Lust, the pagan goddess *Venus*.

The pagans reasoned, "Unbridled sexuality will destroy Christ's name faster than ten thousand arguments. Give us the boys and girls. We will give them sexual license, and the memory of the Cross of Christ shall die. Temples of Venus shall crown every cross of Christ."

Paganism has never changed. It still has one basic attack: lust. Against that diabolical attack, the Holy Spirit has for nineteen hundred years, for one hundred generations, led boys and girls, men and women, to the virtue of Chastity, the control of sexual ap-petite according to the principles of reason and of Faith.

A Realistic Sexual Code

The *U.S. News and World Report* recently had a feature article on the growing incidence of AIDS, herpes, various venereal diseases, pornography, rape, and sexual brutality against women and against children.

During the course of the sexual exposé, the *U.S. News and World Report* did give as one possibility a return to sound sexual morality, but it brushed the possibility aside with the singular comment "we must be realistic."

Yes, we must be realistic. Society must consider the realism that men were made for women and women for men, marriage was made for responsible mothers and fathers, that fornication and adultery and homosexuality and the taking of lives of unborn children, brutalizing women by physical violence, rape, incest, and the sexual abuse of children all are abominations in the eyes of God and in the eyes of all right-thinking human beings.

Our whole society must honor marriage, the family, and responsible sex. This also is a reality, and we must be realistic when we discuss AIDS, herpes, women and child abuse, abortion, and other sexual catastrophes.

Illegitimacy

We are all but surrounded in our society by illegitimate children. I should say we are all but surrounded by illegitimate parents. Because it isn't the children's fault that they are illegitimate, but it is the parents' fault. The census data of the city of St. Louis, just as the census data of most of the central cities in the United States, indicates the average child is born outside of marriage. Single women are now becoming pregnant outside of marrying and even bragging about it. "One-parent families," they now call the illegitimate situation. Individual women on my staff at City Hall had children outside of marriage and continue to have them. What is the solution? There are two basic solutions as I see it:

The scientific evidence must be presented that to have a child outside of marriage is to damage yourself, to damage the deprived child, and to harm society. We must realize that it was God who established marriage and said, "what God has joined together let no man put asunder." As long as we take promiscuity for granted, we must likewise take for granted that we will continue to be surrounded by illegitimate children.

Sex and Sanity

Who of us does not know that the great social problem facing the world today is how to stop the disintegration of the family. Mary, the Mother of Jesus, appeared to a family, the Soubirieux, never known for its sexual rectitude and in a country, France, never known for its sexual propriety. And she identified herself to little Bernadette Soubirieux when she appeared to her eighteen different times, "I am the Immaculate Conception." In stating that she was the Immaculate Conception, she meant that though she was conceived as you and I were through a mother and father, from the first moment of conception, she was without sin.

But the second import of the words "Immaculate Conception" was that she wanted to make sure that all conceptions would be immaculate: to reestablish family life, to bring us back to Christ's doctrine: what God has joined together, let no man put asunder. In affirmation of these apparitions at Lourdes, you may see at Lourdes thousands and thousands of cases of scientifically-ascertainable miraculous cures— the replacing of bones, the iris of an eye, the immediate cure of a cancer, indicating that Our Lady now as at Cana points to Her Son and says, "Whatever He tells you, that you do."

Alcohol and Marriage

Alcohol breaks up more marriages than any other cause. When Judge John A. Sbarbaro of Chicago, who has heard thousands of divorce cases, was asked by news reporters: "What, Judge Sbarabaro, in your experience is the most frequent cause of divorce?" The judge replied without a moment's hesitation: "Alcohol."

It is high time that the danger that excessive drinking offers to the success of a marriage be frankly recognized. In John L. Thomas's famous study of seven thousand broken Catholic families of a Midwestern archdiocese, it was found that not only did drink figure as the number one family destroyer, but that drinking and non-support went hand-in-hand.

In analyzing this fact, Father Thomas stated: "The excessive use of alcohol bears in its train serious consequences for the family. To be specific, alcohol in any form costs money. It is not surprising, therefore, to find that drinking and non-support go hand-in-hand. Further, drinking often leads to physical cruelty and abuse. Another result of drinking is the association with doubtful characters of the opposite sex leading to the presumption of adultery."

Tempting God

There is a famous anecdote of the great St. Augustine. It is told in the masterpiece of autobiography: *The Confessions of St. Augustine.*

St. Augustine wanted to become a Christian. He was convinced that Christianity was true. In order to be received into the Church, he would have to abandon the woman with whom he was living in an illicit union. This woman was not only very dear to him but was likewise the mother of his illegitimate son, Deusdedit.

And so he used to pray: "Dear God, make me chaste —but not yet."

"Dear God, make me chaste —but not yet!" What kind of prayer is this? You expect God to do everything, but we can keep on sinning? Rather we should take the advice of the great St. Ignatius: "Pray as if all depended upon God and act as if all depended upon ourselves."

Lawyers and Marriage Counselors

As in our own day, so in our Lord's day, marriage counselors and lawyers were perplexed by marriage problems and divorce. When our Lord addressed Himself to these marriage counselors and lawyers, He gave them basic principles, which are just as solid today as on the day they were uttered.

To a question concerning serious marriage problems, our Lord replied: "Have you not read, that He who made man from the beginning made them male and female? For this cause a man shall leave his father and mother and shall cleave to his wife and they two shall be one flesh. Therefore now they are not two but one flesh. What, therefore, God hath joined together, let no man put asunder" (Mark 10:5).

Lawyers, marriage counselors, all of us need to ponder the basic principles of our Lord.

1. God not man is the primary Author of marriage.

2. Differences in the sexes have widespread social consequences.

Home Outweighs School

"Well, little man, what do you want to be when you grow up?"

"Please, teacher, I don't want to be anything. I just want to be like Daddy."

And that summarizes the case of us teachers. No matter what we teachers say or do want of our students, when all is said and done, the children want to be just like "daddy and mommy." And I guess that's exactly how it should be.

For the mother and father are the basic professors in the only university that really counts the university of the home. Let me give you an example. Some twenty years ago, I was a teacher of English to first-year high school boys. It was my hopeless task to teach thirteen-year-old boys the difference between "sit" and "set," "lie" and "lay," and various other mysterious words of the English language. But no matter how I would slave to get those boys to repeat after me, "I sit down; but I set the book down," if their parents should happen to say "I set down and I sit the book down," then those students would say exactly what their parents said.

"As the twig is bent, so the tree shall grow." This is true not only in little things, but especially in big things.

Grandparents
Are Very Important Persons

Grandparents are Very Important Persons—real VIPs. I have a letter in my hand from a president. The president is President Lyndon B. Johnson. And the letter is to his grandchild Patrick Lyndon Nu-gent on his first birthday.

"Dear Lyn:

"Today is a very special day for both of us. It marks your first year of life and my first year as a grandfather. It is a role which has given me more joy than any other, and it would not have been possible without you.

"You are my link to the future; you are also my link to the present. In you and through you, I have an even deeper sense of responsibility to all the other children, their mothers and fathers and their grandparents, not just in America but throughout the world. And I devoutly wish for them the happy, fruitful, and ennobling life I wish for you a life free of war, poverty, disease, and inner darkness.

"This I wish, and with God's help, to this I dedicate myself. In the time left to me, I will do everything in my power to make it so. Not just for us in our times but for all men, for all time. God bless you, Grandson. With love, Lyndon B. Johnson."

The Graying of America

When the first census was taken in 1790, half the people in the country were sixteen years old or younger. The United States used to be run by people under fifty years of age, but now it is coming to be run by individuals over fifty years of age.

The Baby Boom of the decade between 1947-1957 produced forty-three million children; we are now coming into the age of the senior boom.

In the next twenty-five years, the twenty-five million Ameri-cans over sixty-five will more than double. In fifteen years, the ten million over seventy-five will more than double.

Medical costs are $3,500 for every elderly person. This is three times the bill for people under sixty-five.

"The average age of persons entering nursing homes is now 80 compared to 70 just a few years ago"—indicating that the health of the elderly is getting better and better.

A Harris Poll found that nearly a third of the nation's over-sixty-five retirees said that if they could, they would still be working.

The Challenge of Old Age:
The Creative Years

The witty French statesman, Talleyrand, remarked about the problem of getting old: "Everyone wants to live long, but no one wants to be old."

Never in the history of the world have so many people lived to be so old. The ancient genii of the Arabian Nights used to promise a long life, but it is the medical geniuses of our day who have brought this gift to us. Just a century ago, the average person had a life expectancy of less than forty years; today living to be eighty and beyond is common. We now have: the challenge of old age as the creative years.

I could tell you about the poet Tennyson who did his greatest work after he was eighty, or the musician Verdi, or the philosopher Kant, or the painter Titian, or Michelangelo, or Anna Mary Robertson, known as Grandma Moses—all of them did great or their greatest work after they were eighty years of age.

How about yourself? Are you preparing yourself for a creative old age?

The Long Life Revolution

We are in the middle of a long life revolution. Never in the history of the world has there been anything like it. The past forty years we have been given an extra twenty-five years of life expectation.

In 1935, when the Social Security Act was enacted by Congress, the average span of life in the United States was sixty-four. Today it is seventy-five. Those who are eighty-five and over are the fastest growing segment of our population. All of us must figure out ways to assist the elderly to stay out of institutions and stay where they want to be—namely within the home. Meals-on-Wheels, in-home services, Visiting Nurses Association all can help. It costs at least $18,000 a year for a nursing home, but for one-tenth of that expense, you can get both Meals-on-Wheels and in-home services. Let's reemphasize for the elderly "Home Sweet Home."

President Ronald Reagan:

The Age Revolution

President Ronald Reagan is a prime example of a revolution the likes of which has not been witnessed in the history of the world. It's called the Age Revolution. Twenty-five years have been added to our life expectancy during the past forty years. The president was just shy of seventy-eight years of age when his term ended in 1989. He was not only the oldest of all of our presidents, he was also one of the healthiest. His height: six-feet-one. His weight: 194. His pulse: 72. His blood pressure 140/80. His cholesterol level 219. "The president continues to enjoy excellent health and has super vigor," reported Dr. Burton Smith, White House physician.

The *Wall Street Journal* did a focus interview of six-year-olds—its conclusion: "The President . . . is widely believed to be forty-two."

When fifty-four-old Walter Mondale injected the age issue into the first of the presidential debates, Ronald Reagan responded: "I am not going to exploit for political purposes my opponent's youth."

"I Came Back to Life"

"A year ago I was ready to die," writes Mrs. Jane Richfield.* "Seventy years of life was enough. My work was over. My family gone. I sat alone lost in memories and self-pity. Then something happened.

"A large noisy family with too many children moved next door. I was polite. But I didn't like it.

"In the weeks that followed, those monsters took on human characteristics. I learned their names. Their heroes. Their hiding places. Their favorite desserts. One day I found myself liking them. The next, loving them. I became the person I'd forgot I was."

Mrs. Jane Richfield, in spite of her age, took on a job as cook at the children's school, and she reports, "I'm doing just fine . . . ." Mrs. Richfield states, and continues, "Older people can give so much if we're given the chance. Without that chance, our lives can be so bleak. So dark. With it, we can become the people we've forgotten we were. We can come back to life."

*Pseudonym: a respondent to the Atlantic Richfield Company's series on the "Involved American."

Secrets of Long Life

A special committee of the House of Representatives wanted to learn the secrets of how to live beyond a hundred. Eighty-five-year-old Chairman Claude Pepper interviewed a number of centenarians. Chairman Pepper pointed out that thirty years earlier there were just 3,000 Americans over 100 years of age, but contemporarily that number was multiplied by seven. The 100-plus group constitutes one of the fastest-growing segments of our society. "Do you want to live over a hundred?" Try these committee conclusions:

1. Be active. If you put your arm in a sling for six months, you'll find out that you can't use it. So likewise with your brain. Either use it or lose it.

2. Diet: Fat people don't have to worry about old age. They'll never reach it.

3. Exercise: Walking, swimming, and dancing seem to be the best forms.

4. Use the common sense that God has given you. And you'll enjoy the gift of life that God has given you.

Youth and Age

Youth and age are probably the most trumpeted non-issue of our time. Many older people have become frightened out of their wits by the totally unreal prospect of being medically "buried alive"; kept alive, that is, in a vegetative condition by extraordinary medical means.

In the first place, if they were in a vegetative condition, they wouldn't know it. . . painful and expensive as the condition might be for relatives. Second, every reputable doctor knows that the quality of life matters —that while he never should fail to try any kind of treatment that might restore normal life, he is practicing bad medicine if he makes the treatment more grievous than the disease or uses extraordinary means to revive someone only to have him or her suffer.

All hospitals—especially Catholic hospitals—have available those "living wills," whereby each of us may state our preference if we simply do not want extraordinary means to be used to restore us to what would be life without quality. I trust in God and go right ahead.

Ice-Floe Ethics

The ice-floe ethics of the Eskimos towards the elderly is well known. When elderly Eskimos could no longer hunt, or sew skins, or build shelters, their relatives would place them on ice floes or otherwise expose them to extinction so as not to diminish the food supply needlessly. Cruel as this may have been, it had community survival value.

But when a society becomes industrialized, when one farmer can feed many people, the practice is an anachronism. Even today, however, many of us insist on placing older people as a group on the ice floes of retirement, in the isolation chambers of rest homes, or on the lonely islands of forgotten living memories.

Friends, ice-floe ethics must cease and the reformation begins with ourselves. An elderly person is made to the image and likeness of God and though his body, as John Brown's body, may be disintegrating and soon lying in the grave, his spirit will go marching on. The elderly deserve our best.

The Old Man and His Grandson

This story is one of the favorites from Grimm's Fairy Tales.

There was once a very old man, whose eyes had become dim, his ears dull of hearing, his knees trembling, and when he sat at the table, he could hardly hold the spoon; he even spilt the broth upon the tablecloth or let it run out of his mouth somewhat. His son and his son's wife were so disgusted at this they would not allow him to eat at their own table but made him sit in a corner behind the stove and eat his food out of an old wooden bowl.

The old man's son and his wife noticed their four-year-old son whittling out a new bowl.

"What are you doing there?" asked the father.

"I am making a new wooden bowl," answered the child, "for you and mother to eat out of when I am big."

The man and his wife looked at each other for a while, and presently began to cry. Then they took the old grandfather to the table, to thenceforth always let him eat with them, and likewise said nothing if he did spill a little of anything.

George Burns

When George Burns was in his nineties, that past decade was his most active. During his eighties, he made seven movies, starred at Carnegie Hall, in TV specials, and nightclubs, wrote several books, and recorded his first country song. When he was asked how he did all of that, his response was: "Magnificently."

A comedian, actor, singer, dancer, a master of living, Burns regarded life as an apple that he wasn't afraid to bite into. "You don't know what you can do unless you do it," George said. "Working and keeping busy is the key. I can't wait to get up in the morning to see what's going to happen." George Burns had come a long way since being born the ninth of twelve children in New York where the family down the road was regarded as well off "because they had curtains on their window."

After the United Motion Picture Association named him entertainer of the century, George Burns cracked: "Wait till you catch me in the next century. . . . I'll be here, I have to be . . . . I'm booked."

Is This Your Old Age?

Jesus said to Peter: "Peter, when you were young, you hitched up your own pants, you buckled up your belt, and you walked wherever you wanted. But when you become old, you are going to have to put out your hands and someone else will put on your belt and lead you where you would not go."

The gospel writer, John, adds: "now this Jesus said to signify by what manner of death he should glorify God. And having spoken thus, Jesus said to Peter: 'Follow me.'"

As we get very old and perhaps are confined to bed rather than hitching up our own pants or buckling our own belts and walking where we want to, someone else—usually a nurse or faithful family member—will help us put out our hands, buckle our belts, and lead us where we would rather not go.

But that wonderful advice given by our Lord to St. Peter is also given to us: "Now this Jesus said to signify by what manner of death Peter should glorify God. And having spoken thus, Jesus said to Peter: 'Follow me.' "

The Myths about Old Age

Myth #1 "You Can't Teach an Old Dog New Tricks"

I have been the Commissioner on Aging for the City of St. Louis for sixteen years, and I have found that there is a whole mythology about the elderly. See if you agree:

Myth Number One: "You can't teach an old dog new tricks."

Perhaps not. I don't know dogs that well. But we're talking about humans, not dogs. I have never seen a healthy older person who could not learn new tricks. You may not be able to teach an old dog new tricks, but "older persons certainly can learn new tricks."

Grandma Moses is classic example of one who switched horses. Born Anna Mary Robertson into a farming family near Greenwich, New York, she married a farm worker and had ten children by him. Bothered by arthritis, at age seventy-six, she gave up her embroidering for painting.

After her first New York showing in 1940, her primitive style quickly caught on, creating a great demand for her works. Grandma Moses continued to produce her popular paintings until her death at ninety-seven years of age.

Older Persons Can Learn New Tricks.

Myth #2 "Old People Can't Keep Track of Family Relationships"

In my sixteen years as Commissioner on Aging for the City of St. Louis, I have found that the second most common myth or lie about old age is that "Old people can't keep track of family relationships."

My experience has been just the opposite. I have found that if there is anything that old folks can remember, it is family relationships.

They can tell you exactly how old Billy and Mary and Ben are; whom Aunt Gertrude married—and what a scoundrel he was—and so on to the third and fourth generations.

When my good mother was eighty-two years of age, she would occasionally forget a name for a moment or two and would say: "I just can't remember his name. It must be my old age." And we brothers and sisters would look at each other in amazement and say. "Mother, join the team. *We* are always forgetting names. Like who was the father of which one of us."

All of us forget names; memory lapse, temporary confusion, momentary preoccupation respects no age limits. Only the nervous systems of the elderly are usually somewhat slower than their younger contemporaries. But old people do keep track of family relationships . . . because these relationships mean so much to them.

Myth #3 "You Can't Do Anything about Getting Old"

In my sixteen years as the Commissioner on Aging for the City of St. Louis, I have found that the third most common myth or social lie is that "you can't do anything about getting old."

That is simply false. It is a lie. You can do something about getting old. First of all you can protect your health by giving up smoking, drugs, excessive use of alcohol; you can investigate and accept a healthy diet and a regime of reasonable exercise.

There was a famous experiment at the University of Minnesota. A physical education professor provided regular exercise to a group of elderly people, all of whom were over seventy years of age. Within two years, these seventy-year-olds had physical constitutions and physical reactions that were normal for individuals thirty-five years of age. Don't fall for the myth, the lie, that you can't do anything about getting old. It is true that you can do no more about the days passing than King Canute could do about the tide rising.

But there are many things we can do about feeling, looking, acting, or being considered *uselessly* old. The chief of these is to keep actively interested in life itself.

Myth #4 "The 'Aging' Are Past Their Prime"

In a real sense, everyone who is alive is aging. The unborn child in his mother's womb; the infant in the stroller, the five-year-old girl in kindergarten, the high school graduate, the butcher, the baker, the candlestick maker—all are aging no matter how young or old they are.

But when we hear the myth that "the "aging' are past their prime," the supposition is that it is only the elderly who are aging and are now useless and all others somehow or other are not aging and are very productive. Pablo Picasso created masterpiece paintings and sketches until well into his nineties; so did Georgia O'Keefe and Titian; Martha Graham at eighty-three was still the master dancer. And what are we to say of Maurice Chevalier, Fred Astaire, Bob Hope, Bing Crosby, Perry Como, Jack Benny, John Wayne, and that whole host of characters and artists who continued their contribution to all of us into their sixties and seventies and eighties.

As George Burns way up in his eighties insisted: "I can't die. I'm booked." Who is to say that anyone is past his or her prime? As Casey Stengel said: "The game ain't over until the game is over."

Myth #5 "The Elderly Don't Fit Into Our Youth Culture"

The myth that the elderly don't fit into the American worship of youth is basically not true. And as our population gets older and older, the myth of the dominance of youth becomes less and less true. Granted that youth used to dominate our American culture, but they no longer do. When the first census was taken in the United States, the average age was sixteen. Thomas Jefferson was only thirty-three when he wrote the Declaration of Independence, and James Madison was only thirty-six when he became the father of the Constitution. Theodore Roosevelt and John Kennedy were only in their forties when they become presidents of the United States. Granted that music and sports and dancing are youth-oriented, but now medicine, political power, and banking have become elderly oriented.

When president Ronald Reagan was seventy-five, he was still going strong.

Our country today is politically dominated by voters over fifty. The Supplemental Security Income Program insures a basic living to every American over sixty-five years of age. Youth are beginning to wonder: Does youth fit into our elderly culture?

Myth #6 "Older People Wish to Be Young"

If you were given the choice of two magic buttons you could push, I wonder which one you would choose? The one says: "I want to live life over again" and the other says: "I don't want to live life over again."

The sexual compulsions, uncertainties, and bungling of our youth are not as comforting as the wisdom, certainties, experiences, and pleasant memories that our older years bring.

In the popular medieval legend, Faust was an old man who so longed to be younger that he sold his soul to the devil in exchange for a fling with the young Marguerita. The brilliant writer Jona-than Swift stated: "No wise man ever wished to be younger."

It seems that as older persons get older, they join in with the Negro spiritual, which sings: "I'm tired of living, but scared of dying, but Old Man River just keeps rolling along." It seems that all of us come to accept the final goodness of Our Lord.

Myth #7 "Old Age and Sickness Go Hand in Hand"

One of the most pernicious myths about old age is that old age and sickness go hand in hand. Old age and sickness do not go hand in hand.

As we grow older, our muscles thin out, but our brains don't and neither does our health. There are only 5 percent of the elderly in hospitals or institutions. The overwhelming majority of the elderly are in good health. Even hundred-year-old persons report in more than 90 percent of the cases that they are in excellent or good or fair health. Only 9 percent report that they are in poor or very poor health.

If you are older, you are more likely to have arthritis, but if you are younger, you are more likely to have measles, mumps, chicken pox, and a whole host of other diseases, especially mental diseases. Despite Alzheimer's disease, a younger person is more likely than an older person to become mentally incapacitated. Sick and injured people are found in every age group. The only thing an elderly (or a younger person) cannot expect is "to live forever" —at least in this life.

Myth #8 "Old Age Is an Illness"

Old age is not an illness. Old age is a perfectly normal development for all of us. The only alternative to dying when we are old is to die when we are young . . . but that doesn't mean that old age is an illness. But some may say: "What about senility? Isn't that a part of growing old?" And the answer is that from a medical viewpoint, "senility" is less diagnosis than a term of abuse. "Dementia in old age is neither general nor common; since it piles up in hospitals, it is visible and frightening."

But as a matter of fact, only one percent of the elderly become demented while three times that percentage afflicts those under sixty-five. If we run out of memory, or thinking ability, or general comfort, it is because we are ill and not because we are old. Incontinence, eccentricity, brain damage, high blood pressure, glandular imbalances, forgetfulness, loss of interest, anxiety, and grumpiness appear in people of all ages. Don't blame it on being old. Thank God for the blessings of old age. And look forward to these blessings.

Myth #9 "When I Get Old, I'll Be Deaf"

If all deaf people were old and all old persons were deaf, then you could truly say: "When I get old, I'll be deaf." But that statement, "When I get old, I'll be deaf," is a myth, it is false.

Deafness is not characteristic and not a necessary concomitant of growing old. But a younger person may say: President Reagan at seventy-five wore a hearing aid and so do many other elderly. And I reply: haven't you noticed how many elderly and how many Japanese wear glasses? Wearing a hearing aid or a pair of glasses really isn't a big deal anymore.

A modern hearing aid is all but unnoticeable and smaller than a dime and glasses make many persons look distinguished or even intelligent. Older persons who hear well are not phenomenal. They are normal. It is all but impossible to find things that apply universally or exclusively to the elderly. The only things that I can think of that apply exclusively to the elderly is that they have been around longer than young people and they have more candles on their birthday cakes.

Myth #10 "Old People Have No Interest in Sex"

Running for re-election several years ago, the United States Senator from South Carolina-seventy-five years of age Strom Thurmond featured his children ages two, four, five, and seven-at political rallies dressed In T-shirts marked "Vote for my Daddy." His thirty-one-year-old wife helped campaign too.

Or take the case of Abraham, the progenitor of both the Jewish and Arab peoples and spiritually the father of us all. When Abraham was eighty-eight, his wife Sarah urged him to have a child by Hagar, a slave girl. The child's name became Ishmael, and later the son of Sarah was Isaac.

The myth and lie that older persons have no interest in sex has an incredible persistence. Why shouldn't older persons be interested in sex, just as they are in food, clothing, shelter, and every other interest of normal human beings? Sex is the intimate sharing of God's own creativity and a stimulus to love. Old people, just like young people, have a healthy interest in sex.

Myth #11 "You Won't Live Long If Your Parents Didn't"

If Winston Churchill, Britain's great World War II prime minister, had taken this myth seriously, he must have had some nervous moments. His father, Randolph, died at age forty-five. His mother, the lovely American-born Jenny, lived longer, until sixty-six. Sir Winston himself, however, died at age ninety-one.

There is some relationship between heredity and longevity. While old age seems to run in families, geneticists are still far from figuring out the connection between genes and longevity. Nor does anyone know for sure just what diet, environment, exercise, degree of stress, or work have to do with length of life. Under no circumstances should we neglect a sensible diet, normal exercise, and relaxation. And if we have a history of a particular problem in the family—heart attack, for example— we should take precautions.

If your parents died young for reasons other than accident or infectious disease, you might too. If they lived to a ripe age, so might you. But it's wise to make no bets either way.

Myth #12 "Thinking Slows Up As You Age"

Brain activity can slow up for a number of reasons: inadequate blood supply, a variety of diseases, lesions, a loss of cells. But cell loss is natural, and even at the normal rate of 100,000 or so a day, it's no matter for concern. At thirty or at seventy, your loss will be about the same every twenty-four hours. At this rate a brain would last more than 550 years. With 15 to 20 billion brain cells in our skull at birth, we can afford the loss of 100,000 per day even though brain cells, unlike others in the body, seem not to be replaceable.

One reason an older person may appear slower in thought process is that when you ask for an opinion, he or she must sift through a large store of experience and data before giving a best answer. If your brain has shrunk, say, 18 percent by the time you're ninety, but you've moved from using 10 percent of it at age thirty to 20 percent at ninety, you're way ahead of the game, provided you've remained free from injury or disease. The point is that brain activity need not slow up or become less efficient because of age.

Myth #13 "Intelligence Declines with Age"

All of us are frightened and fearful of "losing our marbles." Even scientists once believed that intelligence did decline with age. But times have changed and data now reveals that there is no substantial decline of intelligence with age. From a computer-efficiency standpoint, the brain peaks in a person's late twenties. Speed of memorization and calculation then declines slowly with each passing year.

But the skill of solving problems developed over years of living increases, not decreases, with age. An actor learns ways of memorizing accuracy and speed, a businessman builds techniques for trend evaluation and decision-making based on experience, a housewife develops speed and accurate decision-making capability in evaluating prices, foods, and methods of preparing meals. An ability to organize outstrips any decline in brain speed.

The brain is one of God's choicest gifts to you—and you'll find that its power will keep pace with your heart. And they're both lasting longer and longer.

Myth #14 "People Over 65 Are Too Old to Have a Driver's Or a Pilot's License"

There are millions of individuals over sixty-five who are driving cars or piloting planes and are much better drivers or pilots than their younger contemporaries.

Many people over eighty are licensed pilots in powered craft and gliders.

To fly alone or be a pilot in command, you must have a current medical certificate indicating that you are in fit physical shape to pilot a plane. As far as driving a car is concerned, periodic reexamination for drivers of all ages are in order. Reflexes tend to slow down a bit with age, and younger drivers on the whole react more quickly. Unfortunately, though, accidents are not so much related to ability to drive as to such factors as frustration, carelessness, and recklessness, anger and drinking.

Older persons tend to be calmer and more careful at the wheel. They also exhibit better judgment and less tendency toward recklessness. The mythology of aging notwithstanding, you will be safer if you get into a car or plane handled by a licensed senior than one in which a licensed younger person is at the controls.

Myth #15 "If You're Over Fifty and Out of a Job, You Might As Well Give Up"

Here's a common myth that I know is false. The myth states: "If you're over fifty and out of a job, you might as well give up." That statement is a lie.

Yes, jobs is the name of the game. And jobs are available for individuals over fifty. I know it. For fifteen years I have super-vised a program of job placement for individuals over fifty-five, and we have assisted the elderly in hundreds of cases to obtain jobs good—jobs. The experience of age can be a help. At age sixty-five, Colonel Sanders used his first Social Security check to found that massive worldwide fast food chain of Kentucky Fried Chicken.

Why are employers now tending to hire older workers? Older workers have a 20 percent better attendance record, they experience fewer injuries, they get along better with other employees, they appreciate their job more and help company morale, their productivity is high, and their turnover is practically nil. They save you money. If you want an experienced, responsible employee, hire someone over fifty.

Myth #16 "Old People Want to Be with People Their Own Age"

You've heard that myth "Old people want to be with people their own age." Two of my older sisters retired to be with people their own age. They both hated it. They didn't want to be only with older persons.

My one sister, Victoria, retired to her beautiful Ozark lakeside resort home. She soon found herself so confined and use-less that she returned to her former job as being secretary to my brother, the mayor of St. Louis. She wanted to be with a broader spectrum of people. My other sister, Kay, retired when she was over seventy into a retirement home but soon came out of the retirement home because she couldn't stand, as she said: "being only with those older people,"

To those who prefer being with all ages, I suggest that you call your local Area Agency on Aging and ask them about Foster Grandparent Program or the Peace Corps. You remember that Miz Lillian, President Jimmy Carter's mother, at an advanced age, joined the Peace Corps, learned a new language, and went off to India to serve in the Peace Corps for two years. Modern older people seem to prefer the American mix—to be with people of all ages.

Myth #17 "When I Get Old, I'll Have to Live in an Institution"

This myth that you will have to live in an institution when you get old is 80 percent false. Because only 20 percent of our elderly population ever have to live in an institution. Recent scandals involving proprietary or money-making nursing homes have singled out some really horrible examples of abuse and neglect, motivated by greed.

What can you and I do to make life more tolerable for those one out of five elderly who do end up in nursing homes? First recognize that it is possible to cut down on the number of elderly who are all but forced to go into nursing homes. Meals-on-Wheels is one way to help the elderly stay in their own homes. It costs the taxpayer at least $16,000 per year for each person in a nursing home. It costs only $1,000 for a year of Meals-on-Wheels and occasional chore service to help keep the elderly within their own homes.

Your local Visiting Nurses' Association or Area Agency or AARP (American Association of Retired Persons) will tell you how you can help the elderly, help the taxpayer, and help yourself beat that myth: "When I get old, I'll have to live in an institution."

Myth #18 "Old People Are Eccentric"

Every morning when I come to work, I see an eccentric man with a bed roll under his arm and a wild determined look on his face. Quite regularly he puts down his bed roll and either directs an invisible full orchestra or intently plays an invisible violin. He happens to be a young man.

But there is a myth that old people are the eccentrics. There is no evidence that old people are more eccentric than young people. So let's make this plea for tolerance: Different folks, different strokes. Just because I am an American, it doesn't mean that any-thing non-American is no good or odd or eccentric. Just because my skin is somewhat white doesn't mean that someone else who has skin that is somewhat dark is less worthy. Just because I am a Catholic doesn't mean that a Protestant or Jew or Arab loves God and his fellowman any less than I do, or that God loves that person any less. Different folks, different strokes.

Pablo Picasso—at ninety years of age—said that you have to live a long life so that you can be young. Live and let live. Above all, love.

Myth #19 "Retirement Will Kill You"

There is something to be said for this myth that retirement will kill you. Retirement will kill you if you are retiring from your job and have no further interest in life. But if you are retiring to something you've always wanted to do, retirement can be a new lease on life. The gerontological literature establishes this point beyond disbelief: the life expectancy of an older person who enters a nursing home is radically shortened. If the retiree into a nursing home gives up hope, he or she will more probably not live out the shortened 1 1/4-year life expectancy that new nursing home residents have. My mother though a vigorous eighty-four-lasted only two weeks from the day she entered a nursing home.

But if a person retires to new activities and new adventures, such as farming, or painting, or writing, or card playing, or cooking or traveling or volunteering—anything in which he or she has an interest—life expectancy is lengthened measurably. Retirement can kill you, but it need not. It can be the richest time of your life... your golden years. Abandonment kills. Not retirement.

Myth #20 "With Social Security No One Need Worry About Income After Retirement"

Of all the myths about old age In America, there is none greater than the myth about *Social Security* taking care of your old age.

It is extremely important that each of us understands what *Social Security* will and will not take care of.

Only one out of twelve couples and one out of every four retired single or widowed persons rely on Social Security by itself to take care of their retirement. Most people on retirement face the need to make do on half or less than half the income they've been used to. That is a bare, bleak fact of life in America today. As my friend Jack Ossofsky, of the National Council on Aging, has said, "There just ain't much gold in those golden years."

And each of us has to figure out what he or she can do about the fact that Social Security will not by itself take care of old age. Thank God and Uncle Sam for the Supplemental Security Income program with its guarantee of a bareboned poverty minimum for every American sixty-five years of age or older. But that is another story, and to get details, call your local Social Security office.

Myth #21 "The Elderly Need Less"

Who says that the elderly need less? Less of what? Food?

Yes, they can get by on ten to fifteen percent fewer calories because of slower metabolism, but then they have to pay more for

food because they must purchase in small quantities. Do the elderly need less clothing? Not noticeably. What about shelter? Do they need less housing or because of greater vulnerability to cold and heat, do they need better housing? And what about medicine? Do they need less medical care? No, they need more. Three times as much.

The myth of the diminished needs, of adequate Social Security, that old people's dreams, tastes, and expectations somehow shrink and even atrophy—all these promote the idea that the elderly are not an appropriate matter for concern or financial parity because their needs are fewer. Older people are just as interested in their appearance, recreation, pleasant home environments, and food and medicine. Let's wake up. The elderly don't need less. They need better! Beginning with us.

Myth #22 "The Elderly Do Not Need a Family Life"

It's not that grandparents are trying to live with their grown children. Most elderly persons in this country do live close to at least one child, but not under the same roof. "Who wants to spend his life with the big brute of a son-in-law and three teenagers who stay up all night?" one grandmother put it.

A grandmother on welfare says, "I'd rather live alone on practically nothing and be free to come and go as I please."

A public health nurse states: "I hear constant complaints from middle-age children that their mother's places are so messy and their yards full of weeds," she says, "or grandfather needs help be-because he doesn't bathe every day."

These are trivial matters compared to the parent's sense of self-reliance and independence. Tell these people they can't force their own standards on their parents. They must realize that family relations are the most near and dear of those coming to the end of life just as they are those in the very beginning of life. In general, we are what our families are.

Myth #23 "The Elderly Can Get Along Without Love"

Nothing could be further from the truth. No one can get along without love—without becoming mean, bitter, depressed, and rejecting humanity in general and in his own little self.

Love is the freeing of the spirit; it is the goal of life. The poet was at the heart of humanity when he stated, "Ah, sweet mystery of life, at last I've found you . . . for it is love and love alone that rules the world."

When St. John defined Divinity by saying that, "God is love," and St. Paul summarized Christianity by stating, "Love is the fulfillment of the prophets and scripture," they underlined the supreme human and divine truth that mankind is made for love and cannot be happy without it.

The elderly are no different. They must be recognized as complete human beings. They must have others to communicate with. And they must be able to receive and share the seeking of the welfare of another. In a non-formal way, you can adopt an elderly person in your family or allow an elderly person to adopt you. This is one way of ensuring love.

Myth #24 "All Elderly Should Be Put Into Nursing Homes"

"Out of sight, out of mind." It is a frightening thought that perhaps as many as forty percent of the more than a million elderly who are in nursing homes have no medical reason for being there. The reason why they are there is that there is no other place to "warehouse" or "store" them. Hundreds of thousands of elderly who have had a cardiac, a stroke, a major operation, or can no longer shampoo or bathe themselves because of neuritis or arthritis, who cannot give themselves an injection of insulin for diabetes, or are too enfeebled to push a vacuum cleaner or shake out a rug, or go to a store are frequently put into a hospital or a nursing home because there is no other place to go or no one to take care of them.

This is a serious medical, social, and financial mistake. The first day in hospital, even with Medicare, costs a client almost five hundred dollars. Help the elderly to stay right in their own "home sweet home."

Myth #25 "It's Cruel to Talk About Death with an Elderly Person"

One old lady who knew she was dying of cancer received a phone call from her favorite nephew. "I hear you're dying," he said. "I'll miss you."

"Thank you," she replied. "Nobody will talk about it. And I so want to discuss this all-important matter."

Older people normally accept death as the inevitable next step. They often know when they're dying and resent being surrounded by a wall of silence. They want to get things straightened out with God before the last review. To deprive them of the opportunity of discussing what life is all about and what faces them at death is most cruel. By all means make available to the elderly a clergyman of the elderly's choice so that everyone involved may know that the elderly person is coping with his or her death in the best way possible.

What people want most when they're dying is not to be alone. The elderly want companionship in life and in death. Any other indoctrination is a myth.

Myth #26 "If You're Old, You're Bound to Be Ripped Off"

Mr. and Mrs. John Brown took their life's investment and purchased a retirement home in New Mexico, only to find the shopping center that was to be built near their new home and the hospital and the regular community never developed. Their investment was a bankruptcy.

Mrs. Eldoras Smith, sixty-six years of age, purchased land for retirement in Arizona, only to find that her trailer sank in the creek and her home in the mud. Her life savings were gone!

What are we to say about the million elderly who are robbed, mugged, sold worthless policies, real estate deals, home heating and repairs, and promises by creditors of the most vicious sort who view the elders as easy marks?

All we say is "buyer beware." The elderly must be doubly careful. Take every possible precaution. You can beat the myth that every elderly person is bound to be ripped off.

Myth #27 "Old People Die Because They Are Old"

It seems so obvious. But it is a myth. Old people do not die because they are old. As Dr. Hans Selye and other physicians will tell you: "Nobody ever died of old age."

Disease, accident, body abuse, what have you, not old age. Yet we continue to think of age as a cause of death. Old age is not the cause of death but rather stands as a symbol of victory over all forces of destruction, decay, and dissolution that threaten us throughout life.

An older person should be seen first of all as one who received as an unborn baby the priceless gift of life who later was not aborted, who still later escaped becoming an infant-mortality statistic, later a victim of a fatal childhood disease, or an accident in midlife, or a victim of lowered resistance and disorders of later life. A man or woman who has lived to be an old person is actually a triumph, a living symbol of vitality and good fortune and prudent living.

There is a time to live and a time to die, the Scripture tells us. But none of us falls victim to old age.

WOMEN
THE CHANGED ROLE OF WOMEN

We are emerging from a million-year era during which mankind found it functional to give full support to the maternal orientation of the female. No nation could survive unless religion, tradition, and custom reinforced the biologically and economically necessary role of woman as the bearer and rearer of numerous children. Until mod-ern times, continuing childbearing was the essential complement of a high death rate. From birth to death, there was no doubt about the role of the female of the species: She was destined to be a full-time mother. Femininity was identified with maternity.

But all of that has been changed now. The population explosion and the industrial revolution made it imperative that women become equal partners with men in the marketplace and on the assembly line.

How to assure the equality of women and the full care of the fewer children they are bearing is a challenge for all of us.

The Woman's World #1: Finances

We'll never settle this question, but it's good to discuss it. Is this a Woman's World? I maintain that there is a good deal of data to uphold the thesis that this is a woman's world. And in this consideration, I will just take the one field of economics. In general, it is the male who makes the money and the female who spends it. That's a rather favorable division of labor for the woman.

And who owns 55 percent of all stocks and investments? It's the woman.

Who owns 65 percent of all savings accounts? It's the woman. Who owns 70 percent of the private wealth, 80 percent of all life insurance, and spends 90 percent of the family revenue? It's the woman.

Just to prove to you that the woman has this so-called man's world by the throat. . . she buys nine out of ten of the high-grade neckties. So much for the opening salvo in this series on a Woman's World.

Woman's World #2: Physical

Will anyone deny that physically it is a woman's world? She has a more durable body. Science will tell us there are 150 males conceived for every 100 females. Because of the frailty of the male fetus, there are only 105 males born for every 100 females. Newborn girls are much better developed than newborn boys. Males have a 25 percent higher sickness and mortality rate from birth to death.

As far as the physical senses are concerned, men have one half the physical sensitivity, except erotically, that the woman has. Ten times as many men are color blind and 99 out of 100 persons who are near-sighted, and night blind are males. Pity the poor man because physically women are much better off. It is the woman's world.

We have now pointed out economically that it is the woman's world because in general man makes the money and the woman spends it. Now physically, we find it is the woman's world because their bodies are more durable and more beautiful.

As one thief said to another, "Let's take one thing at a time."

Woman's World #3: Emotional

Economically, it is a woman's world because in general men make the money and women spend it; physically it is a woman's world because their bodies are more durable and beautiful.

Now we come to the emotional field. The standard joke is that Edison did not invent the first *talking* machine. The point is women do talk more than men. The reason is they have more to talk about. Why don't the animals talk? Because they have nothing to say. Emotionally, we find women's blood pressure rises twice as much as the male's does. The reason is they have a more sensitive type of nervous system. Their emotion seems to be much more altruistic than men's because they are more critical and appreciative. When you go to the art museum, or a book review, or a play, or a symphony, you will find the clients overwhelmingly female.

As far as being teachers are concerned, there are thirty-five female applicants for being teachers in elementary schools for every male. There is little doubt in anyone's mind that emotionally it is a woman's world.

Woman's World #4: Psychological

We have reviewed the economic, the physical, the emotional, the scientific data concerning the differences of men and women. We came to the conclusion that it is a woman's world.

Now we deal with the psychological. Hundreds of millions of I.Q. tests have been given to boys and girls, men and women, throughout the world. And it is the universal finding that women generally score higher on I.Q. tests than men.

As far as educational achievement is concerned, we find 25 percent more women than men graduate from high school and their grades are higher throughout their educational careers. Women score much higher also on the so-called "intuition." The husband defines this type of "intuition" as that capability a wife has of knowing things for certain that just aren't so. She does have a logic of persons, places, and events, and her accurate and tenacious memory makes it seem that psychologically it is also a woman's world.

Woman's World #5: Field of Religion

Male animals are more difficult to control. The bull is more difficult to control than a cow; the stallion than a mare; the cock than a hen. So likewise with the human species: men are not as capable of being controlled as women are.

Police reports from throughout the world indicate there are roughly ten times as many male criminals as females; there are thirty times as many men in jail than women. Sex surveys, from Kinsey to Masters and Johnson, are unanimous in pointing out that sexually men are in less control than women.

In as far as church attendance is concerned, church is a woman's world. It is the men and not the women who apostatize.

In mixed marriages, it is the man who gives up his religion and not the woman. In general men see the inside of a church when they are hatched and when they are matched and when they are dispatched. If we are to judge the anticipated population of men and women in heaven by the keeping of commandments on earth, it looks as if heaven too is going to be a woman's world.

The Woman's World: Conclusions

From what scientists tell us, this is a woman's world. The economists tell us that women control most of the wealth of the world. The doctors tell us that women are more healthy and live longer. Pediatricians tell us that girls develop two or three years before boys do. Teachers tell us that girls get higher grades than boys do from kindergarten through graduate school. The psychologists tell us that women's psyche is at a higher level than men's; can appreciate more the higher things of life, especially friendship and love. Religionists tell us that the churches are filled with women and the prisons with men. Okay men; it looks like the advertisers are right: "Sell to the women and you will sell to the world."

Magazines are right: "Never underestimate the power of a woman."

The anthropologists are right:

"The mother is the center of civilization."

Psychiatrists are right: "The best way to a man's heart is through the heart of his mother."

The poets are right: "The hand that rocks the cradle is the hand that rules the world."

Until we have data to the contrary, we must conclude it is a woman's world.

SCIENCE AND RELIGION
OVERVIEW: THE NEED FOR LOVE

Modern science increasingly looks to love to solve society's problems. It thereby comes closer to the vision afforded by Judeo-Christian theology. Pitirim Sorokin of Harvard University is an outstanding example of a secular scientist who came to the same general conclusion that only divine love can meet today's social need.

Said Dr. Sorokin: "From the tragic experience of the last few decades, we have begun to learn that without a minimum of love, no social harmony, no peace of mind, no freedom, and no happiness are possible. Partly in this book but more fully in a series of forthcoming studies of the Harvard Research Center... it will be shown that love is literally a life-giving force that altruistic per-sons have on the average a far greater duration of life than ordinary persons; love annuls loneliness and is the best antidote to suicidal tendencies; love-experience is beautiful and beautifies anything it touches; love is goodness itself; love is freedom at its loftiest; love is fearless and is the best remedy for any fear, love is a most creative power; love is an accessible and effective means to a real peace of mind and a supreme happiness; that it is the best therapy against hate, insanity, misery, death and destruction...."

When a secular sociologist such as Sorokin feels that the only ultimate answer to mankind's need of love is the love of God, we have an instance of where science and religion have joined hands, a kiss of peace.

War

War is the greatest social problem of our atomic era. It is the modern problem of survival. The disaster of Chernobyl released atomic particles into the air and threatened the lives of a hundred thousand people. Chernobyl gave us a slight inkling of what might happen should there be another war.

The Bishops of the United States not only warned against the possibility of another war but have stated, "There is an international community of nations. God himself has made the nations interdependent for their full life and growth. It is not therefore a question of creating an international community, but of organizing it."

Scientists agree with this conclusion. One research center stated: "At the present time, there seems to exist no power but creative love that can prevent future suicidal wars and revolutions."

Science and religion join hands saying we must join forces to abolish war.

The Economic Problem

When either social scientists or church people throughout the world speak of "the" social problem, they are speaking of the eco-nomic problem. Church authorities have long stated that the work contract must be modified with some form of "partner-contract... workers and other employees thus become sharers in ownership or management or participate in some fashion in the profits received...." Social scientists and industrial psychologists are coming to the same conclusion. Dr. McMurry, for instance, has concluded from his work for more than a hundred companies that an increase of wages was not the prime interest of the workers. They are striving for recognition as human beings and not as "hands."

The overall findings of the labor specialists highlight that the general principle of love the recognition of the dignity of the in-dividual and the seeking of his welfare-must be reduced to the specifics of economic life if there is to be peace and high productivity. Modern science and theology are at one in analysis and pre-scription in the prime area of economic ailments.

Mental Illness

Every minute a man, woman, or child somewhere in the United States suffers a nervous breakdown. Every two minutes, a man, woman, or child somewhere in the United States enters an institution for treatment of a nervous breakdown. During this current year, some 250,000 people will enter mental hospitals for the first time. There are roughly one million individuals in mental hospitals. Dr. Carl Jung, a co-founder of modern psychiatry, stated:

"I should like to call attention to the following facts. During the past thirty years, people from all the civilized countries of the earth have consulted me. Among all my patients in the second half of life—that is to say, over thirty-five—there has not been one whose problem in the last resort was not that of finding a religious outlook on life. It is safe to say that every one of them fell ill because they had lost that which the living religions of every age have given to their followers, and none of them has been really healed who did not regain his religious outlook.""

Prejudice

If we were to try to summarize the research of the past half-century in the area of bigotry and racial hatred, I suspect that the sentence "There is no hatred but love to hatred turned" would

*Jung, Carl Gustav, *Modern Man In Search of a Soul*, New York: Harcourt, Brace and Co., p. 264.

present closely as any other one sentence the dynamics of hatred as seen by modern science. And I further judge that the sentence "Love begets love" would best summarize the dynamic that re-searchers would most closely agree with as the way out of the jungle of prejudice.

The apartheid hangover in Africa is loathed by both religion and science. The great Harvard psychologist Gordon Allport states why science and religion are allies in seeking to end discrimination:

"One reason why religion is an almost universal attachment of mankind is that religion maintains the basic love relationship of the individual with some embracing principle. The major religions represent not only a free indestructible attachment to one's Creator but likewise the unattained ideal of the brotherhood of man."

Once again religion and science are at one: "Only love will conquer prejudice."

Juvenile Delinquency

Within the next twelve months in the United States, more than one million boys and girls will commit crimes serious enough to cause them to be apprehended by the police. The delinquencies of which our youth are guilty are not mere peccadillos, such as name-calling and curfew violations; in many cases they are brazen and brutal crimes: burglary, arson, vandalism, rape, strong-arming, shoplifting, torture, and murder. In New York, one out of three major crimes involves a juvenile. In Detroit, three of out four car thieves are youngsters.

Social scientists and churchmen now agree on the basic causes and cures for juvenile delinquency.

Family background is number one: most delinquents come from broken homes.

The lack of discipline in the family background is number two. What this means in practical terms is a loving mother backed by a caring father who will insist upon reasonable discipline. There is no known substitute for a loving mother backed by a firm and caring father.

Infants Without Love

If you would understand the highly dramatic way how necessary love is, even on an organic level, we should consider infants without love. Parents may readily realize that if a child is deprived of love, he will probably die. Non-parents may not realize this. The world-famous child psychiatrist, Dr. Rene A. Spitz, has scientifically demonstrated the importance of love, even from a purely organic and survival level. Throughout his long career, Dr. Spitz has been doing research on the need of love in the infant's life. In his film called *Grief,* Dr. Spitz records the tragic story of infants in a South American foundling home.

Infants without love, infants deprived of love have a 50/50 chance of dying. The world-famous child psychiatrist, Dr. Rene Spitz, points out in the documentary film *Grief,* that when infants in foundling homes are deprived of love, they become frustrated and tense. This turns to panic, rage, hate, aggression, exhaustion, withdrawal, mental and organic disintegration, and in many cases death itself.

English psychiatrist John Bowlby of the World Health Organization found in his studies on the lack of love on children: "Children who suffer deprivation grow up lacking the capacity to care for their own children. Deprived children are a source of social infection as real and serious as the carriers of diphtheria and typhoid."

The name of the disease that children radically deprived of love suffer is called Marasmus, "the wasting away of the body because of the lack of love." Life itself is dependent upon love.

Alcoholism

Alcoholics Anonymous groups meet all over the country. If you should attend Alcoholics Anonymous meetings, as I have with my alcoholic father, you will be surprised as I was by several features:

These men and women are in earnest. They are fighting for their sanity, they are fighting for their jobs, their homes, their salvation.

The Alcoholics Anonymous program is a spiritual pro-gram. It has twelve steps, and every one of them declares the alcoholic's dependence on God and his fellowmen. "We admit that by ourselves we are powerless; We have come to believe that a power greater than ourselves can restore us to sanity, we have made a decision to turn our will and our lives over to God as we understand Him. We shall live in thankful contemplation of Him who presides over us all."

Thank God for the Alcoholics Anonymous program. We can all profit by making an act of dependence upon God and our fellowman.

Solitary Confinement

If we needed proof from religion or science that human beings disintegrate unless they have companionship and love, all we would have to do is look at the horrors of solitary confinement. (The worst punishment for convicts is not physical punishment of whip or chain or inadequate food but solitary confinement.)

Ex-convict Arthur Barry gives us an insight into the horrors of loneliness as experienced during his year's stretch of solitary confinement: "And so I spent 23 hours a day in that 6 by 8 foot cell. Always I had to fight the impulse to scream or bang my head against the wall... I saw about twenty men taken out of isolation some in straightjackets-in a state of screaming insanity. But there was another form of escape. A man would lapse into what is known as 'prison stupor,' which is living death. Failing to keep his mind active, the prisoner retreats into the past and gradually loses contact with reality. In prison lingo, he is 'ready for the straw hat'—the mental institution." Companionship and love are necessary for life itself.

Social Problems
The Social Security Act

Without doubt, the Social Security Act, signed into law on August 14, 1935, is President Franklin D. Roosevelt's most important domestic achievement and most lasting legacy—"the greatest democratic revolution in our history," says noted historian Henry Steele Commager.

Born out of the Great Depression, its guiding principles remain essentially the same as they were in 1935: to assure that elderly (and later disabled) citizens have a guaranteed income against the day when they can no longer work, and to avoid attaching that stigma of welfare to those in need by making the program nearly universal in its scope. The unfinished revolution of the Social Security Act is to enact a national health-insurance plan for all citizens and to treat elderly women, particularly the widows, on an equal basis as males are treated. The Social Security Act is as tri-umph of Democracy.

Immigrants

To the Jews, Samaritans were unwelcome foreigners and immigrants. And so when Jesus even spoke to the Samaritan woman by the well or told the story of the "Good" Samaritan, the Apostles were scandalized. They thought that Jesus should not do business with nor welcome such "foreigners" and "immigrants." There are two myths about immigrants to our own country that should be exploded:

Myth #1: Immigrants Are a Burden on Taxpayers. The fact is: federal study reveals that within ten years of their arrival, immigrant families begin to earn more than the average native-born American family.

Myth #2: Immigrants Live on Welfare. Fact: According to U.S. Census Bureau statistics, the average immigrant pays about $1,500 more in taxes than he receives in public benefits. Friends, immigrants, just as your own immigrant ancestors, become good American tax-paying citizens.

"I Was a Stranger..."

The Statue of Liberty means a great deal to all of us.... Weren't your ancestors immigrants?

You can return the favor by helping the latest arrivals adjust to their new country.

Here are some ideas:

Welcome immigrants into your community. Greet them when you meet them in church or on the street. Cultivate respect for the language, customs, and traditions of other people. Brush up on American history and the part that ethnics played in it.

If others disparage ethnics, don't join in. Instead, talk about contributions that ethnics have made to the United States. Learn about your own roots, your own ethnic background. Introduce ethnic customs in your own household.

Keep up with world affairs, and learn why people are leaving their homelands.

Volunteer to work an organization that helps immigrants re-settle or teach English as a second language.

These are practical ways of fulfilling Jesus' Last Judgment scene: "I was a stranger and you welcomed me."

Mexico

Mexico is of growing importance to all America. We cannot understand the strength of Mexico without understanding the meaning of Our Lady of Guadalupe. In a country steeped in the racism and the pride of blood of Spain, Our Blessed Lady appeared at Guadalupe. She came not as a pure-blooded Aryan or lily-white-faced Nordic or a high-blooded Spaniard, but appeared herself as a lowly native maiden to a poor discredited half-breed Indian.

And hanging above the main altar of the Basilica of Our Lady of Guadalupe, you may inspect the miraculous life-size picture that Mary has left of herself. It's lovely Indian features imprinted on the peasant worker's apron reemphasized Christ's doctrine that there is no longer slave nor free, no longer Jew or Greek, male or female. But we are all one in Christ Jesus Our Lord.

Communism's Mortal Enemy

Almost seventy years before the atomic disaster of Chernobyl in Russia, on October 13, 1917 in the town of Fatima in Portugal, there was another forbidding physical Phenomenon. The atheist editor of the anarchist Portuguese newspaper O Seculo was one of the 70,000 witnesses. He wrote an account of the vision of Our Lady and the sun. He stated that "the sun danced."

To the three children of Fatima, Lucy, Francis, and Jacinta, our Lady gave an even more terrifying vision than that of the fire of heaven. She showed them the fire of hell. She asked for the establishment throughout the world devotion to her Immaculate Heart and communion in Reparation and stated, "if my requests are heard, Russia will be converted, there will be peace. Otherwise, great errors will spread throughout the world ... wars, persecution, martyrdom, and nations will be destroyed; but in the end, my Immaculate Heart will triumph and an era of peace will be con-ceded to humanity."

Three Myths of the Poor

Myths—as the poor are with us always. But here are three myths about the poor that we should investigate and squash.

Myth #1: Poor people refuse to work. This is a myth. Most poor— (and there are 34 million of them in the United States) are children. Of the 7.3 million families living in poverty, more than half have at least one worker. And there are 1.4 million able-bodied seeking work but were unable to find it.

Myth #2: Most poor are black. This is false. Two-thirds of the 34 million poor are white and fewer than 10 million are black.

Myth #3: The business boom was helping all the poor. This is

a myth. There were a growing number of poor, even during the recent business boom. The rich were getting richer and the poor were getting poorer. What can each of us do about this growing polarization between the rich and the poor? Study the issues and vote wisely.

Is Politics a Dirty Word?

"Politics" is a dirty word in many people's dictionaries. But in my *Webster's* dictionary, it is not a dirty word. Politics is there defined as "the art or science of government." Yet strangely enough, the term "politician" is held in great disdain. It is generally considered that a politician is a cunning, conniving, dishonest individual, not interested in the common good but only in his own aggrandizement.

According to a famous Gallup poll, it was discovered that mothers all would be pleased if their sons or daughters would grow up and become president of the United States; but three out of four States; but three out of four of these same mothers do not want their children to become politicians in the process. They do not realize that a president is the chief politician in the process. For the president or elected chief of state must win over the people to vote him into the highest office of the country.

Pope Pius XI had this to say about politics: "The domain of politics, which concerns the interests of society as a whole, is the field of the widest charity, of political charity, of which it may be said that there is none above it, save that of religion.

The field of politics is democracy in action and can be a way for you to do good for others.

What Does the Laboring Man Want?

Dr. Robert McMurry is one of the world's modern leaders of industrial psychology. After studying more than a hundred companies, Dr. McMurry has concluded that an increase of wages is not the prime interest of workers. They are striving for recognition as human beings and not as "hands"; employees lack identification with their companies, and they are seeking their place as important partners in the economic processes. Employees prefer jobs that are "free from condescension and overclose supervision; that give free play to their talents; that give credit for work done; that allow them to participate in decisions affecting themselves, that bring together small teams of congenial co-workers; and that permit personal growth and advancement."

Both modern theology and modern industry are at one. The recognition of the dignity of the individual and the seeking of his welfare, must be reduced to the specifics of economic life if there is to be peace and productivity. A full day's work for a full day's pay is good religion, good business, and good employer-employee relations.

"Race: The Unfinished Revolution"

ABC Television's "PRIMETIME LIVE" had a great idea. Match up two individuals in everything except race and see how differently they are treated. ABC telecaster Diane Sawyer was given the job. She chose two handsome young men of the same age, same weight, same height, same education, same family background, they even played on the same softball team—only one, John Kunnen, was white, and the other, Glenn Brewer, was African-American, black.

Diane, John, Glenn, and an ABC TV sound and video crew went off to a typical Midwestern city, St. Louis, to see for a national audience whether there really was any difference in the way Americans received a white and a black.

First, they went into a department store. With microphone and camera hidden, John the white went up to the counter to be waited on. He was greeted by the clerk in a very sociable manner and was immediately waited upon. A minute later, Glenn, the black, went up to the counter was not waited upon and in fact was indirectly insulted by being tracked as if he were a potential shoplifter. It was the same story when they went apartment hunting. The white was given complete access and encouragement; the black was told that there were no more apartments available. Purchasing a car: yes to the white; no to the black. Both by plan were locked out of their cars. The white was given help and encouragement by a whole circle of well-wishers; the black was left alone; and shunned as if he were a leper or AIDS contaminated. Whether asking for street directions or seeking a job, the same story was true: the white was welcomed, the black was rejected! Is this what it means to be a black in America?

Jesus Christ re-emphasized that every human being is made to the image and likeness of God, that whatever we do to another, Christ takes as done to Himself, that love for others—especially the disadvantaged—is the sign whereby we can be identified as His followers, that we are no longer Jew or Gentile, slave nor free, male nor female, but we are all one in Christ Jesus our Lord.

Building upon this truth that God has created all of us equal and given each of us inalienable rights, our founding fathers began the American Revolution. That Christ revolution, that American revolution must continue in our own lives. We can declare to ourselves and to our own little world our one person affirmative-action revolution. Blacks have made great progress since the Declaration of Independence. But accenting blacks as our real equals is the unfinished American Revolution.

CHRISTOLOGY
WHAT IS JESUS–GOD OR MAN?

It was at one of her delightful dinners for university professors that Charlotte Zimmerman, the wife of my good friend Professor Carl Zimmerman, asked me, "Lu, do you really believe that Jesus was God?"

"It is completely unscientific," I said to this group of university professors and their wives, "It is completely unscientific to say that Jesus was not God but that he was a good and intelligent man like Socrates, and Buddha, and Muhammad, Lao-tzu, Confucius and Mahatma Gandhi: I find that even naturally speaking from a purely scientific viewpoint it is much more logical to admit that Jesus was God. A lunatic could not produce the world's greatest literature. A liar could not invent the world's greatest system of truth and then choose to be tortured to death for what he knew to be a damnable lie."

"Before Abraham was, I am," said Jesus to the Scripture scholars who knew God by the name "He who Is" —"I and the Father, are One," declared Jesus.

"One Solitary Life": Jesus of Nazareth

An unknown writer stated: *Here is a Man* who was born in an obscure village, the child of a peasant woman. He grew up in an other obscure village. He worked in a carpenter shop until He was thirty, and then for three years, He was an itinerant preacher. He never wrote a book. He never held an office. He never owned a home. He never had a family. He never went to college. He never put His foot inside a big city. He never traveled two hundred miles from the place where He was born.

While still a young man, the tide of popular opinion turned against Him. His friends ran away. One of them denied Him. He was turned over to His enemies. And when He was dead, He was taken down from the cross and laid in a borrowed grave through the pity of a friend.

Nineteen wide centuries have come and gone, and today He is the centerpiece of the human race and the leader of the column of progress.

I am far within the mark when I say that all the armies that ever marched, and all the navies that ever were built, and all the parliaments and Kings and Presidents that ever reigned put together have not affected the life of man upon this earth as powerfully as has that One Solitary Life.

World's Ten Greatest Personalities

"Name the ten greatest personalities in the history of the world." This was the question asked by the *American Mercury of* H.G. Wells, the noted atheist, author of *An Outline of The History of the World.*

H.G. Wells replied, "There have not been ten great personalities in the history of the world. There has been only one great personality: Jesus of Nazareth."

And this is true. Even from a natural viewpoint. That world-famous leader of men, Napoleon Bonaparte, noted the same. Napoleon offhandedly remarked: "Alexander the Great, Caesar, Charlemagne and I founded kingdoms on force. But Jesus Christ founded a kingdom on love. Today there are millions all over the world who would at a minute's notice leap into the jaws of death out of love for Him. But there is not one would die for love of me."

And the same is true today. Christ has not changed; He still dominates the world of human beings whether they will accept Him as divine or not. Jesus Christ—yesterday, today, and forever the same.

The Jordan Management Consultants Report

If Jesus had submitted the résumés from the twelve men whom He had picked to head up the massive organization and op-eration that He proposed, He well might have received the follow-ing report:

TO: Jesus, Son of Joseph
           Woodcrafters Carpenter Shop
           Nazareth 25922

From: Jordan Management Consultants

Dear Sir:

Thank you for submitting the résumés for the twelve men whom you have picked for management positions in your new organization. All of them have now taken our battery of tests, and we have not only run the tests through our computer, but also arranged personal interviews for each of them with our psychologist and vocational aptitude consultants. The profiles of all tests are included, and you'll want to study each of them carefully.

As part of our services for your guidance, we make some general comments. It is the staff's opinion that most of our nominees are lacking in background, education, and vocational aptitudes for the type of enterprise that you are undertaking. They do not have the team concept. We would recommend that you continue your search for persons of experience in managerial ability and proven capabilities.

Sincerely,

Jordan Management Consultants

A Letter to: Jesus, Son of Joseph—Woodcrafters Carpenter Shop—Nazareth 25922

From: Jordan Management Consultants

The Management Consultants evaluation of the twelve men whom Jesus picked as His apostles might have concluded with the following statements:

Simon Peter is emotionally unstable and given to fits of temper.

Andrew has absolutely no qualities of leadership.

The two brothers—James and John—the sons of Zebedee, place personal interests above company loyalty.

Thomas demonstrates a questioning attitude that would tend to undermine morale.

We feel it is our duty to tell you that Matthew has been blacklisted by the Greater Jerusalem Better Business Bureau. James, the son of Alphaeus, and Thaddaeus definitely have radical leanings, and they both registered a high score on the manic-depressive scale.

One of the candidates, however, shows great potential. He is the man of ability and resourcefulness, meets people well, has a keen business mind, and has contacts in high places. He is highly motivated, ambitious, and responsible. We recommend Judas Iscariot as your comptroller and right-hand man. All of the other profiles are self-explanatory.

Signed: Jordan Management Consultants

St. Peter and Judas

If we compare Peter and Judas, we cannot help but be im-pressed by the fact that both Peter and Judas were apostles of Christ; both had listened to Christ's words, both had seen His mir-acles and both had betrayed Christ—the one with a kiss, the other with a curse; and both were sorry that they had sinned. So sorry that the one had hung himself with a halter around his neck and the other—well, let me put it in the words of a little girl who had been asked by the nun: "Mary Jane, what would you have done if you had been Judas and had sinned as he did?" The little girl solemnly replied: "If I had sinned as Judas had sinned, I too would have hung myself... but around the neck of Jesus."

And there is the difference between Judas and Peter. Both had sinned, both were sorry, and both, as it were, hung themselves. But Peter became a saint by hanging himself around the neck of Jesus. He knew God's mercy is bigger than any sin of man. "His mercy is above all of His works."

When Your Faith Is Put to the Test

The apostle Peter's faith was tested when he and the other apostles boarded a boat at sundown and were crossing the Sea of Galilee. Suddenly there arose a dangerous storm. It was now night; the sea raged, the wind howled, the little boat was tossed about. When all seemed lost, Jesus came to them walking upon the sea. And the Apostles seeing Him were frightened and cried in fear. Jesus spoke to them, saying: "Fear not, it is I."

Peter, hearing the voice of His Master, said, "If it be Thou, bid me to come to Thee upon the waters."

And Jesus said: "Come." Trusting in Jesus, Peter felt nothing impossible, so he walked toward Jesus. Then suddenly he looked away from Jesus; trusting in his own power, he began to sink.

Realizing that his trust in himself would be disaster, he looked to Jesus and cried out: "Lord, save me."

Jesus stretched out His hand, grasped Peter's hand, and said, "Oh, thou of little faith."

Friends—when our faith is tried, Jesus Christ stretches out His hand to us.

"Fear not, it is I," he says. "Come."

"Because She Has Loved Much"

Thank God, that Mary Magdala was such a big sinner. Yes, I am happy that Mary Magdala committed so many sins, was a woman of the streets, a professional sinner. Because by the very fact that Mary Magdala was a prostitute and became such a close friend of both Jesus and Mary, never again can any of us doubt that God's mercy is above all his works.

The Lord tells us if your sins be as scarlet, they shall be made white as snow, and if they be red as crimson, they shall be white as wool. He tells us that it is the sick and not the healthy who need the physician. "I have not come," He says, "to call the just, but the sinners."

Mary Magdala, the sinner become saint, dramatizes for us that there are two kinds of people who can love God with their whole heart and their whole soul and their whole mind. The first type are those who love God because they have never left him. The second type are those who love God because they once left Him and found their way back. There is room for both types in the great Heart of God.

The Most Important Part of the Story

A man hurrying along a busy city street stopped before a church-good store window to stare at an arresting picture of the crucifixion. So absorbed was he that it was several minutes before he was aware of a small boy standing beside him. The little boy was looking at the picture with an attention that matched his own. "Can you tell me, sonny, what that is all about?" he asked, seeking to draw the lad out. "Doncha" know?" The boy marveled at the man's ignorance. "Why, that's Jesus, and those others is Roman soldiers, and that's His Mother Mary standing over there crying. and..." he hesitated, "they killed Him."

With something in him satisfied, the man hurried on down the street. Soon he heard pattering footsteps, and the little boy rushed up beside him. "But I haven't told you the most important part of it all yet," he said breathlessly. "He rose again and He's now in Heaven."

That little boy was absolutely right. The most important part of the story of the crucifixion is not the crucifixion, but our Lord rose again and is now in

Heaven where we can join him.

The Wonder of the Mass

Life Magazine remarked about the wonder of the Mass: "Every minute of every day in one of 200,000 Catholic Churches all over the world, a priest is saying Mass. Every Sunday and on specified feast days, every Catholic must attend Mass. Every Catholic means more than one half billion persons in the world or one out of every five persons now alive and more than fifty million people in the United States alone. Thus the Mass, always the same every-where, is the most universal of all the world's religious dramas."

Life Magazine's commenting that "Every minute of every day in one of 200,000 Catholic Churches all over the world, the Mass is in progress" highlights the prophecy of Malachias who foretold the wonder of the Sacrifice of the Mass in these words: "From the rising of the sun, even to the setting thereof, My name shall be great among the Gentiles, and in every place there will be sacrifice, and a clean oblation shall be offered in My name, saith the Lord God of hosts."

Jesus Christ, and His Mass, yesterday, today, and forever the same.

What Is the Mass All About?

"What is Mass all about? — What do you Catholics do at Mass?" And when my good friend Dr. Carl Zimmerman, a Harvard professor, asked this question at a family dinner in Cambridge, everyone stopped talking, for they likewise were interested in finding out what the Mass is all about.

My answer is very simple. The Mass is the continuation of the Last Supper. Let us find out what Jesus did at the Last Supper. Jesus did three things: Scripture tells us that there was the Offer-tory: "And taking bread, He gave thanks." In other words, He offered the bread and wine to God. Secondly, Scripture tells us there was the Consecration: He changed the bread and wine into His Body and Blood by saying: "This is My Body, which shall be de-livered for you.... This is My Blood, which shall be shed for you." And thirdly, there was the Communion: "Take you and eat."

And here we have the essentials of every Mass: from the first one in the Cenacle or Upper Room of the Last Supper almost two thousand years ago, to the last one today in the parish church... Offertory, Consecration, Communion.

Going My Way

It was Bing Crosby who made this gracious statement about the priests and nuns: "We've each got our little spot in this big movie of life, and the trick is to play our part the way the Great Director wants it played. Most of us are spotted to places like mine—with a bunch of youngsters and a good wife at home to pro-vide for. But some of us can move up into really big star roles, if we answer the call when the Great Director goes about casting. The important thing is to have studied our abilities and to know whether or not we can play the roles which are opened to us. For me (continues Bing Crosby) I envy the boy who gets called up for a life-long starring as a Father O'Malley or a girl starring as Sister Benedict. In my book, they are the ones whose names are going to stand first on the program, spelled out in capital letters, and in good black type. In my book, these are the stars."

Will Women Ever Be Priests?

There is the story of Pope John Paul II being in an ecstasy prayer and God spoke to him. "Is there anything that you would like to know?" God asked the Pope.

"Well," said the Pope, "yes, I would like to know if women will ever be priests?"

God responded to John Paul: "Not while you're alive.... Is there anything else that you would like to know?"

"Will we ever have another Polish Pope?" blurted out John Paul.

Without hesitation God responded: "Not while I am alive."

Friends, I'm not interested in whether or not we'll have an-other Polish Pope, but I am interested in whether or not women will ever be priests. The progress report of the story seems accurate... we certainly will not have Roman Catholic women priests while the present Pope is alive. He has indicated that though there is nothing theologically unacceptable in women becoming priests, historical precedent does not justify it. A recent national survey indicates that there has been an upsurge of Catholics who wish women to be accepted as priests. Almost fifty percent in the poll agree. I too agree.

God is Spirit. God is neither male nor female. In Christ there is neither male nor female.

Our Little Crosses

At Mantua in Spain, when anybody has been killed, they bring the corpse into the central square and make each citizen come up and place his left hand upon the body, raise his right hand, and say, "I swear to God I had nothing to do with the slaying of this innocent person." I wonder, if we took the Body of Our Lord down from the cross and placed it there on the lap of Mary... I wonder if there is anybody who could come up and, placing his left hand upon the Body of Christ, could raise his right hand and say, "I swear to God, I had nothing to do with the death of this innocent person."

You and I know that we could not do that. As Mary untwines that thorned crown from the Head of her Son, you and I recognize that if it had not been for the sins of the world and our sins, Christ would not have died. With Mary, we empathize with Our Lord and recognize that we can offer our daily little crosses with the big cross of Jesus for the salvation of souls.

"What Does It Profit...?"

An elderly man walked into a crowded gambling house in a Western city, sat down at a roulette table, and placed a few chips on number 34. The wheel spun, slowed, and stopped.

"Number 34, red. There you are, sir," intoned the croupier. The old man did not twitch a muscle. He sat leaning over the table motionless, the chips were left on 34. The wheel was spun again. "Number 34, red," the croupier announced.... Five more times Number 34 red won and then the croupier calmly called for "silence" and announced, "Sorry, ladies and gentlemen, but there will be no further betting tonight. The casino is closed."

Turning to the old man, he said, "You have broken the bank, sir, please collect, you—" he halted in wide-eyed astonishment.

Only then did he realize why the old man had neither moved nor spoken since the first spin of the wheel.

A dead man had broken the bank. "What does it profit a man if he gains the whole world, but suffer the loss if his immortal soul?"

Hallowed Be Thy Name

Once upon a time— so this story goes—once upon a time, a priest overheard a lad of eight or nine using the name of God in vain. "Johnny, you should not use God's name like that," re-marked the priest, to which

Johnny quickly replied: "But, Father, you use God's name in vain too." "Oh, no, I don't," the priest retorted. "And I'll bet you anything you want that I never take God's name in vain." But the lad was convinced he was right and bet the priest an apple pie.

Three Sundays later, Johnny was at Mass. It was time for the homily. The priest began with the solemn words: "By God we live, by God we die," and Johnny jumped up and said: "Yes, and by God, you owe me an apple pie."

Friends, an apple pie or not, we all know that we should not use God's name in vain. The next time you should use God's name in vain, do what I know they do in one Hollywood studio. Make yourself give five dollars or more to your favorite charity each time it happens. You'll soon get over using God's name in vain.

Parable of the Good Samaritan

We all know the parable of the Good Samaritan. Jesus told this story of how a certain man was going down a treacherous road from Jerusalem to Jericho and was set upon by robbers who beat him, robbed him, and went their way, leaving him half dead.

We remember how the story continues by saying that first one priest and then another priest just passed him by, but at length, the good Samaritan, a man of another culture, another land, came along, took compassion on the victim, bound up his wounds, took him to an innkeeper, gave him money, and said: "Take care of him; whatever more thou spendest, I, on my way back, will repay thee."

I heard of a very young nun who was suddenly asked by her little first-grade students: "Sister, what kind of priests were those—passing by that poor robbed man so that he would die in the road?" The Sister was flustered, but she recovered her compo-sure by quickly answering: "Well, you see, those weren't *real* priests; they were just Jesuits."

Being a Jesuit myself, I solemnly affirm that such is not the point of the story.

Hell

Hell is a very controversial topic. A woman sent this question to her newspaper. "My husband keeps telling me to go to hell. Do I have the legal right to take the children?"

A Texan was defending his state as the greatest in the union by saying: "There's nothing wrong with Texas that some water and some good people wouldn't cure." His non-Texan friend retorted: "And there's nothing wrong with hell that some water and some good people wouldn't cure."

When anyone asks me if a good God could condemn anyone to hell for all eternity, I have to agree God's mercy is above all of His works. Consider the Last Judgment to have a panel of three judges: God the Father says the soul is saved. The devil says that soul will be damned. The individual himself decides which way his soul shall go. Each of us with the grace of God is the master of his or her own destiny.

Dr. Robert Hutchins speaks of "the good news of damnation." Hell is good news because it has peopled heaven. As crabs, we back away from fire, and by backing away from the fires of hell, we fall into heaven. If there were no good hell, possibly there would be no good Christians.

Mistaken Identity

A dispatch from the United Press stated that a Mrs. James Peters of Riddle Lake, Indiana, dove off a dock at Riddle Lake to save the life of a drowning four-year-old lad only to find out that the person she had helped to save was none other than her own son, Jimmy. The incident of the heroic Mrs. James Peters assisting an unknown person only to find out that the person she helped was someone quite different and precious is very much in line with the classic stories of mistaken identity: "The man dressed in rags, with whom the poor peasants shared their food, turned out to be none other than the king; the down and outer the wayfarer helped turns out to be a millionaire; the girl the hero saved turns out to be his sweetheart; the emergency case is the doctor's own son."

In a real sense, the theme of mistaken identity is the story of our own lives: because our Lord tells us that at the Last Judgment, each of us will be informed that whatever we did to another, we did to Him: "Whatever you did for one of these, the least of My brethren, you did for Me."

Power of Prayer

No one who falls upon his knees in prayer does not rise a better and a stronger person. Above the doors of the Church of Our Lady of Guadalupe in Mexico City, you may read the simple in-scription: "Enter a good person, leave a better one."

The poet Tennyson recognized the mighty power of prayer when he had his hero, the dying King Arthur, say: "More things are wrought by prayer than this world dreams of."

One of the century's greatest scientists, Nobel prize winner Dr. Alexis Carrel had this to say about prayer: "As a physician, I have seen men and women after all other therapy had failed, lifted out of disease and melancholy by the serene effort of prayer. When we pray, we link ourselves with the inexhaustible motive power that spins the universe. Even in asking, our human deficiencies are filled, and we arise strengthened and repaired." So speaks the scientist, Dr. Carrel.

"Knock and it shall be opened to you, seek and you shall find; ask and it will be given to you," says our Lord.

Mother of God

A certain St. Louis woman was irritated at hearing so much honor given to Mary as the Mother of God. She complained to her Catholic neighbor: "I don't know where you get all this Mary stuff. Mary's a mother and I'm a mother, and there's no difference between us." To which her neighbor softly replied, "... Mary's a mother, and you're a mother, and there's no difference between you... but there is quite a difference between your sons."

And there is the critical point. According to the Scriptures, Christ is truly God; He is equally Son of Mary. The Son of Mary and the Son of God are one and the same person. Mary is therefore Mother of God, not as if Christ owed His divinity to her-that would be absurd and blasphemous-but because Jesus Christ, is only one Person and this Person is God.

A comparison with ordinary motherhood will help. When a human child comes into being, God creates his soul, and the union of body and soul forms a new human person. Yet no woman con-siders herself mother merely of the flesh and blood of her child. She is mother of the new person. So likewise Mary is the mother of the God-Man. Mother of God.

Entertaining Bad Thoughts

An eight-year-old boy was trying to get his conscience straight. He told the pastor: "Father, I have bad thoughts." To which the priest replied: "I have bad thoughts too. Everybody does. But that does not mean you have sinned. Did you entertain those evil thoughts?" The little lad thought for a moment and re-peated: "Did I entertain my evil thoughts? No, I didn't entertain *them*, they entertained *me*."

This lad's reply, "I didn't entertain them, they entertained me," brings out the basic distinction: thinking is not willing. All types of evil thoughts automatically enter everyone's mind: lying. murder, drunkenness, rape, slander, theft, fornication, and all of these thoughts may be entertaining—appealing to my senses—but until I entertain them willfully, there is no sin.

When Catherine of Siena was tempted by continuous evil thoughts for three days and our Lord finally appeared to her, she asked Him: "Lord, where were you when I was all but overwhelmed by all those evil thoughts?" To which our Lord softly replied: "I was there in the middle of your heart or you would never have been able to resist the temptations."

Serenity of Soul

Here is a beautiful and simple story, which one of you listeners sent to me. This story is called "God's Trees." It is about a whole family of discontented trees in the time of our Lord. One of these trees was chosen by the Roman soldiers to become the cross upon which our Savior was crucified. It was this tree that had become a cross that heard at 3:00 PM. on the First Good Friday, the bloody and battered Messiah exclaim, "Father, into thy hands I commend my spirit." And the cross, which as a tree was so discontented, now obtained a peace and serenity of soul.

He had begun to understand. God has his plans for each of us.

And out on the hillside, all the trees of the forest family bowed their heads and thanked God because their brother, the cross, had found the secret of serenity of soul. "God's will be done." This is peace and joy of soul.

Prayer and Work

There is a story told of a little girl who was brought to Church for the first time. Seeing all the men and women kneeling, she asked: "Daddy, what are they doing?" To which her father quietly answered: "They are saying their prayers." The little girl could not believe it and she all but shouted: "Saying their prayers... with all their clothes on!"

However, this little girl was no more wrong in thinking that one can pray only at home in one's night clothes, than those who think that one can pray only at church in one's Sunday clothes. God tells us, "Let nothing hinder us from praying always" (Ecclesiasticus 17:24).

Jesus bids us, "Watch ye therefore, praying at all times." "Whether you eat or drink, or do anything else, do all for the glory of God," says St. Paul (1 Cor. 10:31). Very obviously we cannot be praying vocally all the time. Our lips cannot be moving in prayer while we are eating or sleeping or working. But we can raise our hearts and minds to God. And we can do this, somewhat contrary to what the little girl thought, with all of our clothes on.

The Greatest Story Ever Told

I believe the all-time greatest story that has ever been told is the story of the last judgment. It is a story about you-about you and the way you treat your family and friends and all with whom you come in contact. Here's how the story goes:

It is the end of the world, and the last judgment of each one has arrived. All mankind has been gathered together from the four winds. Jesus Christ, the only Son of the eternal God, has come in all His majesty. See Him standing there. Jesus, at the throne of His Father, calls out to those at His right Hand: "Come," He says, "come, you blessed of My Father, take possession of the Kingdom prepared for you from the foundation of the world; for I was hun-gry and you gave Me to eat; I was thirsty and you gave Me to drink; I was a stranger and you took Me in; sick and you visited Me...."

That's the greatest story of all times; however we treat others, God takes as treating Himself.

PERSONALITIES
BILL COSBY

Have you ever watched *The Cosby Show*? It was a U.S. phenomenon. Thirty million people watched Bill Cosby once a week.

Who then is Bill Cosby? William Henry Cosby, Jr. was born in 1937 in Philadelphia: his mother worked as a housemaid and his father was gone most of the time. That's quite a different background from that of the "doctor" father and "lawyer" mother and their five children having such a terrific time in his Cosby Show TV family.

Bill Cosby created the show because in real life he does have five children. And he didn't like the type of TV shows that his children were watching: ugliness and violence. People on TV never seemed to be having a good time. Most importantly, Bill Cosby knew there was no television show that showed a loving black family. The show was a great success, and from the first, it was the number-one-rated series on television. This says something highly favorable not only about Bill Cosby but about the American people who choose to watch the show. When you are tempted to think America has gone to the dogs, I suggest that you take a look at *The Cosby Show* and see that everything is working out just all right.

Danny Thomas, Comedian

Danny Thomas's baptismal name was Amos Jacobs, but for thirty-five years, he has been known as Danny Thomas, the "King of the Comedians."

As one of ten children, he lived in a miserable cold-water flat.

He remembers his brother was bitten by a rat and was about to die. His mother made a vow that if he recovered, she would devote one year of her life going from door to door in Toledo, Ohio, begging pennies and nickels for the poor. The boy lived and his mother kept her vow.

Something similar happened to Danny. At twenty-six years, he was a down-and-outer. He wandered into the Church of Saints Peter and Paul and knelt before a statue of Saint Jude.

"I remember very clearly," Danny Thomas says, "the vow I took, I said, 'Please help me find my way. And I'll build a shrine for the helpless and the lost and the hopeless. If I'm not meant for show business, give me some sign and I'll get out. But if I am meant for show business, then I'm gonna stay and try to make it all the way.....'"

Danny made it all the way, and his shrine was built.

Jim Ready's Mother

Do you want to hear a story of double heroism? It is the story of a St. Louis University student by the name of Jim Ready. Jim went to the help of a friend of his as they were coming out of a Cardinal baseball game. His friend was attacked by a drunken rowdy. Jim went to his help, and within minutes, Jim Ready was dead. A rusty switchblade knife had pierced his heart.

And here is the double heroism. At the time of the funeral, Jim's mother stated: "My boy Jim lived with malice toward none. And now it is as if he has handed this down to us as his legacy. We feel no bitterness towards those who caused his death... Jim died performing an act of charity and in so doing, he revealed the charity burning in hearts of countless numbers of fellow men who reach out to share our sorrow. The loss of a life so beautiful must surely bring greater beauty into our world. If and when hatred can be replaced with love," the slain boy's mother concluded, "our loss will be redeemed."

Harpo Marx

Superstitions and Seances

Does your rabbit's foot bring you good luck? That rabbit's foot didn't bring the rabbit good luck.

Are fortune tellers, spiritists, mediums in league with the devil?

The great Houdini claimed that there was no seance that he

could not reproduce by natural means by trickery-and he proved his claim in a score of cases. Harpo Marx upset a seance in Hollywood when he asked to talk with George Washington.

After a long pause, the medium said in a spooky voice: "George Washington is now listening. What question do you want him to answer?"

Harpo Marx said: "Please, George Washington, tell me what is the capital of North Dakota." When the supposed George Washington, father of our country, couldn't answer the question, "What is the capital of North Dakota" for the simple reason that the spook medium didn't know the name of the capital of North Dakota, everybody broke out laughing.

Some American coins state: "In God we trust." This is the best way to replace superstitions and seances.

Dr. Charles E. Sajour

A Story of Forgiveness

Dr. Charles E. Sajour of the University of Pennsylvania cured a seven-year-old girl who had been suddenly stricken dumb. Dr. Sajour found out that the father, a poor Lithuanian tailor, had surprisingly struck his daughter in the face. The child had not spoken since. Dr. Sajour brought Elizabeth into his office and said: "It will be very simple to correct this trouble, so long as you forgive one another, and, Elizabeth, my dear, this is not going to hurt except for the moment. I am going to give you a slight shock from an electric battery, and your nerves will react properly. Do you understand?"

Elizabeth nodded that she did and after Dr. Sajour had laid a small disk attached to a cord against the small white throat, Elizabeth recovered and stated in a small childish voice: "Daddy, it's all gone. And you didn't mean to slap me."

As explained by Dr. Sajour, there was no electric shock, and when Elizabeth was able to forgive, she was able to talk. "It merely helped her to express herself," stated Dr. Sajour.

Richard Baillar

Three days before Christmas, Richard Baillar's mother asked Richard to shine her good shoes for her. Shortly after, with the prideful smile that only a seven-year-old can muster, Richard pre-sented the shoes for inspection. Pleased with the results, his mother rewarded him with a quarter.

On Christmas Day, as she put on her shoes to go to church, she noticed a lump in one shoe. Taking it off, she found a quarter wrapped in paper. Written on the paper in a child's scrawl were these words: "I done it for love." Friends:

When the song of the angels is stilled,
When the star in the sky is gone,
When the kings and princes are home,
When the shepherds are back with their flock,
The work of Christmas begins:
To find the lost,

To heal the broken,
To feed the hungry,
To release the prisoner,
To rebuild the nations,
To bring peace among brothers,
To make music in the heart.

Christophers

A Christopher is defined as a bearer of Christ. Here are six examples:

1. A bus driver surprises his passengers by being pleasant under all circumstances.

2. A housewife makes it a practice to write letters of protest when she comes across things that are offensive in the press, radio, or movies. She is careful to make each letter kindly, respectful, and constructive. She sends letters of praise where praise is due.

3. A businessman chooses, even at a small salary, a position or a leading magazine that "breeds paganism." He has already helped to change its policy a little.

4. An office worker sends information, pamphlets, and books to persons in key positions.

5. A salesgirl changes from a job selling hats to one selling books. She awakens one day to the fact that books affect the inside of the head, while hats affect only the outside.

6. A nurse in a large public hospital helps dying patients, no matter what their religion, recite an act of sorrow for their sins.

A Football Physician The Power of Suggestions

This is a true story of the power of suggestion. It was at the Monterey Park football stadium in Los Angeles. During half-time a number of persons reported symptoms of food poisoning. The staff physician found that they had all used a soft-drink-dispensing machine under the stands.

The doctor panicked. Because he felt a responsibility to everyone in the crowded stands, he had an announcement made that no one was to use the dispensing machine under the stands be-cause a number of fans had become ill, and the symptoms were described.

The minute that the announcement was made, the entire stadium became a sea of retching and fainting people, including many who had not gone near the dispensing machine. Hundreds fled the stadium. Five hospital ambulances had to race back and forth between the emergency rooms. Two hundred people were hospitalized.

Then the doctor found that the soft drink machine had nothing to do with the original illness. And the moment when it was announced that the soft drink had nothing to do with the problem, everyone suddenly and mysteriously recovered, just as before they had become mysteriously ill.

The Traveler and the Bell

For Whom Does the Bell Toll?

There is the famous story of the traveler and the bell. One morning a traveler came upon an old man who was very sad and one who was sobbing to himself. The traveler was moved with pity

and stopped to ask the old man: "Can I help you?" "It's the bell," muttered the old man. And the traveler listened. Sure enough. From a distant church steeple, the slow mournful toll of the funeral knell was beating out its sad refrain.

"Oh, I'm very sorry," said the traveler, "I take it that the bell is ringing for the death of one of your friends or relatives?"

"Worse than that," murmured the old man.

"Then the bell is tolling for one of your own family?" The old man slowly shook his head and still woefully muttered,

"Worse than that."

"Worse than that?" exclaimed the traveler, "How can that be? Tell me then: for whom does the bell toll?"

Then the old man looked up, and with tear-dimmed eyes, he replied: "For whom does the bell toll? It tolls for you and for me!"

Three Workers

Your Work Is Valuable

The famous medieval story of the three workers can give us a better understanding of the worth of work. There was a traveler who once came upon three men who were doing identical work on a rock pile. The stranger asked the first worker: "What are you doing there?" The reply: "I am breaking up stones."

Later he asked the second worker: "And what are you doing?" "I am making stones the right size for building purposes," replied the second worker.

Finally, the stranger asked the third man what he was doing and the answer was, "I am building a cathedral."

All three workers were doing the identical work, but only one worker realized the true worth of his work. This story has its application for you and me.

No matter what type of work you do, you likewise are building a cathedral you are doing God's work. The simple fact of our work is this:

God made the earth and all things on it, but He has handed over the mechanism for you and me to carry on. Our work is the continuation of God's work. We are His Partners.

The Blood Donor

There's the story of a young lad from Cincinnati who over-heard his father saying that his older brother needed a blood transfusion immediately. The youngster thought it over awhile, and though he wasn't quite sure what these "blood transfusions" were, he asked his father, "Dad, can't I give Bud the blood transfusion?" The parents thought it over, and soon the mother was taking the boy to the clinic.

Within fifteen minutes, the nurse had removed the half-pint of blood that was needed. The boy's jaw was set, even though he was shuddering a bit. He raised his manly tear-dimmed eyes to his mother and quietly asked, "Mom, do I die now?"

That mother almost fainted when it became clear how brave her boy had been. With a burst of love, she drew his slightly pro-testing form to herself as she realized that he had thought he was giving his life so that his brother might live!

"Greater love than this no one hath than he lay down his life for his fellowman."

Norman Cousins

The Therapy of Joy

There is a true story of a newly used, low-cost therapy. A therapy of joy. It is being used with cancer-patient support groups at the Sepulveda Veterans Administration Hospital. Whatever the clinical reasons, it is well known that an upbeat attitude enhances the chances of medical success for any therapy. In this particular support group, Norman Cousins introduced a "therapy of joy." Every veteran was to bring in weekly anything good, anything joyous, anything upbeat that happened to him during the past week.

One veteran began the next meeting by saying that his good news was that he had contacted a buddy whom he hadn't been able to reach for twenty years. There was polite applause. Another said that he had received an unexpected IRS check from the federal government (there was wild applause).

Another said that on an airline trip back to Los Angeles, his bag had been first off the carousel (and there was jolly laughter).

Friends, joy and a positive attitude are among the best medicines known to humanity. How about bringing a joyous story or anecdote back to your home tonight?

Self-Improvement
The Hunchback King

Here is an ancient legend about a hunch-backed, bitter and mean king. One day a sculptor came to the court and asked permission to carve an image of the king's head.

"Do me from head to foot," ordered the king. "But without my curse—do me as I might have been."

The sculptor was in love with his remarkable task, and when he had completed his magnificent and perfect statue, the king commanded, "Put it in the secret grove, beside the pool at the bottom of the garden."

For years every day, the king went to the secret grove and stood for hours, contemplating the statue of his ideal self.

By and by people began to ask: "What has come over our ruler? How he has changed!"

These whispers came to the king's ears, and he hastened at once to the secret grove. Standing beside the still waters, he looked down upon his image reflected in its depths. And he saw that his back was straight, he stood erect, and he was like the marble image of his ideal self.

The Kingdom of God Is Within You

There is an old Hindu legend that deserves retelling. "In the beginning," so this legend goes, "all men were god-like in their nature. But man sinned against the godhead of which he was possessed and so lost this wonderful gift. Brahma, the Lord God of all, assembled the lesser gods about him and asked: "Where shall we hide the godhead from man so that he will not find it and mis-use it again?"

One of the lesser gods suggested that he hide the godhead on top of the highest mountain while others suggested he bury it deep in the earth.

"No," said Brahma, "because man is ingenious and will find ways to get to the highest mountain and down into the lowest depths of the earth and so find the godhead to misuse it again.

"I will tell you," said Brahma, "Hide It Deep Down in Man Himself: He Will Never Think to Look There."

The Hindu legend was right: The Kingdom of God is within you.

First Concentrate

Arturo Toscanini, the late great conductor, was once walking through a passageway of the Metropolitan Opera on his way to the stage to conduct Beethoven's *Fifth Symphony* when some thoughtless fan interrupted his train of thought, held out a pro-gram, and said: "Mr. Toscanini, how about signing this?"

Mr. Toscanini did. But then he went back to his room to recollect himself for another fifteen minutes. He had been distracted, and he knew that without uninterrupted thought about what he was going to do, he could not do it well.

This is a sound psychological maxim. You have to concentrate, think about what you are going to do, or you cannot do it well. The distinguished American, Captain Eddie Rickenbacker, in his autobiography, *I believe in Prayer* stated: "Think positively and masterfully, with confidence and faith, and life becomes richer in achievement and experience." Similarly with prayer. You have to think beforehand what you are about to do or you will have a difficult or impossible time in doing it.

As Scripture tells us: "Before prayer prepare thy soul and be not as a person that tempteth God" (Eccles. 18:23).

A Series of Smiles

This is the story of how a series of smiles was born. The series of smiles started on the lips of a Swedish girl who was working at a news stand in a San Francisco hotel. When patrons bought papers or magazines, she usually took their money in the most casual and perfunctory manner. She said an impersonal "thank you," and turned to the next customer. This girl had the most bewitching and friendly of smiles, but she rarely let it be seen.

One fine day her pastor, Father Michaels, tackled the delicate subject. "You have a wonderful smile, Ingrid Swenson, one that could cheer many a person who may be carrying a heavy burden. Don't make God sorry He didn't give that smile to someone who would use it."

It was a revelation for the news stand girl. From that day on, she gave every living creature a smile. She let her inner cheerful-ness be reflected in her eyes, her voice, the lift of her head-and she reaped a heartful of happiness for herself.

What about you and me today?

The Other Key

Hugh Downs tells of a young man who was named in the will of a rich uncle. The uncle left him a job in one of his banks, plus the contents of a safe-deposit box in one of the bank's vaults. Two keys were required to open the box—one was provided him when the will was read, the other he had to find for himself.

The young man frantically searched for the other key, reasoning that his uncle had set a test for him deeming him worthy only if he solved the problem. He reread the will, questioned relatives, and studied his uncle's life and papers to find a clue. But there was no real clue.

There were many false clues and false hopes through the years, and as time wore on, he despaired. As one last attempt, however, he decided just to use the key that he had all along. Imagine his surprise that the bank safe-deposit box could be opened by the one key that he had had all along. His uncle had wanted him to know that the other key, as most of our rules and regulations, are not necessary; all we have to do is use resources that we already have... that's the other key.

Self-Incarceration and Self-Emancipation

Mark Twain once told of a man who languished for years in a dismal dungeon, scheming how to get out by tunneling under-ground, prying out of a high window, or cutting through the wall. Suddenly he rose, opened the door, and walked out to freedom. The door wasn't locked after all. He merely had to determine to open the door!

It may be that the plight of many of us is similar. We conclude there is nothing that we can do to correct some condition that is imprisoning us, whether it is alcoholism, smoking, drug dependency, cursing, or going with some one we know is detrimental to our own well-being. We read self-help books, expecting that this will hand us an instant solution, or we go to doctors and say, "Cure me."

These procedures do not work. Suddenly you rise, open the door, and walk out to freedom. You smell the fresh air of freedom because you yourself determine that you will smell the fresh air of freedom.

Thinking Can Make You Well

There's a book called Psych neural Immunology, edited by Dr. Robert Alder of the University of Rochester. It reveals the connection between psychological factors and disease. It shows the roles of psychological factors, for example, in bringing on cancer, hearing diseases, rheumatoid arthritis, and even infectious diseases. Medical science has finally become able to pierce some of the mysteries—the mechanisms that relate psychological factors to disease and health.

It is now established, for instance, that prolonged depression or despair can actually impair the immune system. Scientists have been able to show that people in a state of prolonged depression and despair have lower levels of "natural killer" cells in their immune system than those who are not depressed. Conversely, per-sons who can visualize good things happening to them actually activate those good things happening to them within their physical systems.

These discoveries have broad ramifications in the lives of each of us.

One Day at a Time

Everything was going wrong. It was during the sixth game of the World Series being played in St. Louis between the National League Champions, the St. Louis Cardinals, and the American League Champions, The Detroit Tigers. Despite the fact that the St. Louis Cardinals were the heavy favorites to win the series, they had just been bombed out by the Detroit Tigers 13 to 1 in one of the most humiliating defeats in the long history of World Series classics.

Bob Gibson, known as "Baseball's Best Pitcher," had a sore arm. It was known that he did not want to pitch the seventh and final game: "The biggest day of the season." And it did turn out to be a catastrophe for the Cardinals and a triumph for the Tigers. But no matter how much the fans and the media harried Bob Gibson about the evil possibilities of tomorrow, he always said: "One Day at a Time. Today is the biggest day of the season."

And this is how he made his meteoric rise from the ghetto to glory: One day at a time. Today I will do my best. The angels themselves can do no more.

Mental Health

Hollywood's Sam Goldwyn stated: "Anyone who would go to a psychiatrist ought to have his head examined."

One out of two of the beds of this country is covered by individuals who are mentally rather than organically ill. We would all do well to examine the basic principles of our life and make sure that we keep our heads on straight.

Whenever a little boy in Catechism class replies "I am a creature composed of body and soul and made to the image and like-ness of God," he has established a self-identity that not a million dollars worth of psychiatry, however valid, could supply. The seven-year-old girl who knows that "God made me to know Him, to love Him, to serve Him, in this life and to be happy with Him forever in Heaven" will never have to worry about whether she's coming or going. Her mental health is secure.

And if you will latch on our Lord's commandment of love, your mental health is quite secure: "A new commandment I give you: that you love one another, as I have loved you."

A Substitute for Herman Forsythe

The following letter was sent to me as a joke. I hope that the letter will be more of a joke to you than a reality. The letter reads: "Dear Friend: Perhaps you have heard of me and my nationwide campaign in the cause of temperance. Each year, for the past four-teen years, I have made a tour of our nation and delivered a series of lectures on the Evil of Drinking. On these tours I have been ac-companied by a young man, a friend and assistant, Herman Forsythe.

"Herman was a pathetic case, a young man of good family and excellent background, whose life was ruined because of excessive indulgence in whiskey, gin, and rum. Herman would appear with me at my lectures, and sit on the platform drooling at the mouth and staring at the audience through bleary, bloodshot eyes, while I would point him out as an example of what drink would do.

"Unfortunately, last summer poor Herman died. A mutual friend has given me your name and I wonder if you would care to accompany me on my summer tour and take poor Herman's place."

The Vision of Sir Launfal

We have all been captivated by the story of Sir Launfal's search for the Holy Grail—that cup out of which Christ drank with His disciples at the Last Supper. Sir Launfal spent most of his proud warrior life in search for that chalice; he wanted something worthwhile that he could present to Christ. But he was unsuccessful in his quest.

After several years of fruitless searching, he returned down-cast, heartbroken, and poor to his castle home. As he approached the entrance to his home, he saw an unkempt beggar standing there; the beggar put out his hand and said: "In the name of Christ, will you help me?" The once-proud Launfal would now pay attention even to this poor man, and although he had but half a loaf of bread, he gave that to the beggar.

But as he was handing the bread to the poor man, behold—he saw in those eyes and that face not the features of a beggar—but the face of Christ.

Not in some foreign land, but right at his own front door, Sir Launfal finds salvation.

Robert Bruce, King of the Scottish Chieftains

On his deathbed, the Crusader King Robert Bruce of Scot-land told his Lieutenant Douglas to bury his heart in far-off Jerusalem. After Robert Bruce died, Douglas took the heart of his king, placed it in a large golden locket, and with a cord hung it about his neck.

It was at a crucial battle against the Saracens that Douglas's Christian troops were about to be overrun. It was then that Douglas reached for the cord about his neck and drew forth the golden casing containing the heart of the king. He held it high in the golden light of the setting sun and hurled it into the midst of the enemy, calling out to his fellow fighters: "On, brave soldiers, after the heart of our king!" The Christians routed the Muslims and won the day, following the heart of their king.

Friends, our enemies during this day may well be Saracens of personal selfishness, greed, pride, lust, and despair. We too can overcome our enemies by following the heart of our King.

In and Out

It was a hot, uncomfortable day in St. Louis, and the line at the post office was long and slow-moving. As I waited my turn, I marveled at the patience of the woman behind the window. She had a pleasant smile for everyone, in spite of all the complaints about the heat, the slow mail-delivery service, and the high postal rates. At last my turn came. I was about to ask this mail clerk how she maintained her serenity in the face of so much opposition when I noticed the small black earrings she wore. One of the black earrings in white lettering had inscribed the word "In"; on the other, "Out."

You have heard a great deal about paying close attention to what everyone says and really thinking it through. But on things that are negative or scandalous, I suggest that you too wear small black earrings either actually or figuratively: on one in white lettering should be inscribed "In"; and on the other, "Out." "In" and "Out" can be the name of the patience game.

The Seventy-two-Second Personality Course

Here is a seventy-two-second personality course:

1. The first rule is to use the word "you" in conversation and not "I";

95

2. The second rule is even simpler: Smile when you speak—a smile is more important than lipstick. And you men: it takes more muscles in your face to frown than to smile. Relax and you'll make others relax. Be pleasant and you'll find others are pleasant. Research indicates that blood pressure of a person goes down when in the presence of a dog that is wagging his tail.

3. The third rule refers to the content of your conversation: get a man to talk about his work, a woman to talk about her problems. Who doesn't want to talk about what she or he is interested in?

4. The fourth rule is: Stay alive, be interesting, read, observe. The greatest form of love is to be interested in others.

The rules for developing our personality are identical with the rules for developing your love for mankind and for God.

The Waldorf-Astoria

A man in the Bible once entertained certain strangers in his home and did not find out until after they had left him that they were messengers of God.

A young man by the name of George C. Boldt was a clerk at a small hotel in Philadelphia when an elderly couple entered the lobby. They had no baggage. "Every guest room is taken," said the clerk, "but still I can't send a nice couple like you out into the rain at one o'clock in the morning. Would you perhaps be willing to sleep in my room?... Oh, I'll make out just fine; don't worry about me."

Next morning, as he paid his bill, the elderly man said to the clerk: "You are the kind of manager who should be the boss of the best hotel in the United States. Maybe someday I'll build one for you!"

Ten years later that old man and his wife did build the most beautiful famous hotel of its day, the original Waldorf-Astoria. He made that young clerk, George C. Boldt, its general manager.

We should treat well all strangers who seek our help. Their ragged coats may hide their wings!

"Only When I Laugh"

It was back in the Wild West days of the Indians and the scouts. Two good scouts were after a bad, bad Indian. They knew that he was in the woods somewhere. So they agreed to separate and the first scout would go one way and the second scout the other way, to meet back in camp in one day.

But three days went by and the first scout did not return. The second scout went out to get him and finally found him, but he was pinned to the trunk of a tree still living but with a huge arrow right through his middle. The second scout looked at him and exclaimed: "You've been this way for two days?"

"Yes," muttered the first scout.

"And all this blood lost? And no water? And the bugs biting you. And the arrow right through you. Doesn't it hurt?"

"No," bravely gasped the victim, "only when I laugh!"

Friends, that story is a bit way out. But there's a grain of truth in that tall tale. Don't groan out loud. Don't cry and spread your

gloom on all those around you. Our Lord tells us that even when we fast, we should put the oil of joy on our face and greet our fellow-travelers with a smile. Give your little cross to our Lord as a partnership with His Big Cross. And you know: "God loves a cheerful giver."

Aesop's Fables
The Belly and Its Members

You heard this story by Aesop "The Belly and the Members" when you were a child. I think it will mean more to you now since you are an adult. Social Solidarity is its theme:

In former days, Aesop's fable begins, when all a man's limbs did not work together as well as they do now, but each had a will and a way of its own, the Members began to find fault with the belly for spending a useless life, while they were wholly occupied in laboring for its support. So they entered into a conspiracy to cut off its supplies for the future. The Hands were no longer to carry food to the Mouth; the Mouth was not to accept food; the Teeth were not to chew food.

They had not long continued in this course of starving the Belly into subjection, before they all began, one by one, to fail and flag, and the whole body began to pine away. Then the Members were convinced that the Belly also, cumbersome and dark and use-less as it seemed, had an important function of its own, that they could no more do without it than it could do without them, and that if they would have the constitution of the body in a healthy state, they must work together, for the common good of all.

A Donkey Carrying Salt

Aesop has this famous story of the donkey who was forced by his master to carry heavy salt to the market. The donkey accidentally slipped and fell into the waters of the river one day, and so much of the salt was washed away that the load was much lighter. The next day he decided to slip and fall on purpose. The master then decided to show that lazy donkey "He can't play tricks on me."

The next time the shopkeeper went to the sea, he bought a quantity of sponges and filled the donkey's basket.

"Not so heavy this time," said the donkey to himself. "By the time I've washed this lot away, I'll have no load at all."

But when the donkey fell again in the river, hoping for his load to be washed away, the sponges filled with water and got heavier.

Oh, dear, thought the donkey, something's wrong here. The load in my basket is weighing me down.

He called for help from his master, who said, "That'll teach you to play tricks with me," and he led the poor struggling donkey home where he almost collapsed with exhaustion.

Aesop's moral: "Don't try to be too clever; it may rebound on you."

The Fox and the Goat

By an unlucky chance, a Fox fell into a deep well from which he could not get out. A Goat passed by shortly afterwards and asked the Fox what he was doing down there. "Oh, have you not heard?" said the Fox. "There is going to be a great drought, so I jumped down here in order to have water by me. Why don't you come down too?"

The Goat thought well of this advice and jumped down into the well. But the Fox immediately jumped on her back, and by putting his foot on her long horns, managed to jump up to the edge of the well.

"Good-bye, friend," said the Fox; "remember next time, 'Never trust the advice of a man in difficulties.' "

If we ask ourselves how do we balance off the admonition of Christ to do unto others as we would have done unto ourselves and the fable of Aesop that we should never trust the advice of a man in difficulties, the answer seems easier if we recognize that the words of Jesus must be within the frame of reference of common sense. The advice of a man in difficulties is less than trustworthy.

The Wolf in Sheep's Clothing

A wolf decided that he had had enough of being hunted and shot at. So he thought up a plan that would ensure that he had plenty to eat without having to work too hard for it. "If I wrap myself in sheepskin and slip in among the sheep, no one will notice me." So he took the skin of a dead sheep and covered himself with it, making sure to hide his gray body. Then he joined the sheep and was shut up at night with them in their pen.

When it was quiet, he decided he would like fat sheep for dinner. Unfortunately for the wolf, the shepherd had the same idea. The Shepherd went to the pen to kill a sheep, taking a sharp knife with him. Because it was dark, the shepherd grabbed the first sheep that he could find. But the sheep that he killed turned out to be a wolf. Imagine his surprise!

And Aesop concludes with this moral: Never pretend to be someone else.

The Fox and the Lion and The Lion and the Statue

When first the Fox saw the Lion, he was terribly frightened. He ran away and hid himself in the woods. Next time, however, he came near the King of Beasts, he stopped at a safe distance and watched him pass by. The third time they came near one another, the Fox went straight up to the Lion and passed the time of day with him, asking him how his family was, and when he would have the pleasure of seeing him again; then turning his tail, he parted from the Lion without much ceremony.

Aesop's conclusion: "Familiarity breeds contempt."

Then there's another fable by Aesop in which a man is dis-cussing with a lion the relative strength of men and lions in general. The man contended that he and his fellows were stronger than lions by reason of their greater intelligence.

"Come now with me," he cried, "and I will soon prove that I am right." So he took him into the public gardens and showed him a statue of Hercules overcoming the lion and tearing his mouth in two.

"That is all very well," said the Lion, "but it proves nothing. for it was man who made the statue."

Aesop's conclusion: "We can easily represent things as we wish them to be."

The Vain Crow

There was once a crow who was so conceited he thought he was much better looking than his friends and relations. He thought he was every bit as beautiful as the peacock on the terrace.

One day he found some peacock feathers lying on the ground. He picked out the most gaudy of them and stuck them amongst his own black ones. Then he began strutting about, showing off his borrowed plumes to the peacocks. He really did look like quite a beautiful bird. But it didn't take the peacocks long to find out that he wasn't one of them, and they set upon him, pecking at him and stripping his borrowed feathers with their sharp beaks and taking many of his own feathers out as well.

The crow was so ashamed of his bald patches that he scrambled back to his own patch where the other crows were waiting.

"Go moult with the chickens," they chorused. "You're too good for us, or so you said."

Aesop's conclusion: Don't despise your friends; you may need them one day.

Aesop said we should not despise our friends because we may need them one day. He had no way of knowing that our Bible would say that we shouldn't despise anyone because every person is made in the image and likeness of God.

The Goose That Laid the Golden Eggs

Perhaps there is no more famous fable than that of "The Goose that Laid the Golden Eggs." A farmer and his wife once bought a goose at the fair. Imagine their surprise when they brought it home and the first day it laid a solid gold egg. They couldn't believe their luck. But it happened the next day and the next until it was laying golden eggs every day of the week.

Instead of being grateful for their good fortune, they began to get greedy. The farmer's wife said to her husband, "One egg a day is all very well, but we won't get rich fast enough that way. Why don't we cut the goose open and get all the gold that she obviously has inside her?"

The farmer wasn't very happy about killing the goose because it had brought them good fortune. But his wife insisted. So he cut open the goose and what did he find? Nothing, no gold at all. She was just like any other goose. Now they wouldn't get rich at all, and they had cut off their daily supply of gold.

Concludes Aesop: "Be thankful for what you've already got."

The Monkey and the Dolphin

Aesop tells us there was once a pet monkey who lived on board a ship and was fed and taught tricks by the sailors. The monkey was very clever and knew ways of getting round the sailors to give him extra food.

One night a great storm broke out. The ship tossed from side to side and great waves rose over it until at last the ship capsized. The sailors tried to save their pet, but the monkey was swept away. He was splashing great mouthfuls of salty sea when he was spied by a dolphin. Quickly the dolphin swam to his aid and took him on his back towards the shore.

"This is the coast of England," the dolphin told the monkey. "Do you come from there?"

"Of course," said the monkey, "I come from one of the best English families."

"Ah," said the dolphin, "then you'll know Plymouth well."

The monkey laughed. "Of course I do. He's one of my best friends."

The dolphin was so disgusted at the monkey pretending to have rich friends that he dived under the water and left the monkey to swim to the shore alone, which he did, but only after a great struggle.

Aesop's conclusion: "Your lies will always be found out."

The Lion and the Rabbit

"One day a lion was sauntering along when he found a rabbit asleep in the grass," said Aesop the slave in one of his famous fables.

"Hm!" he said to himself, "a tasty nibble before I have a proper lunch." He was just about to eat the rabbit when he saw a deer run past.

Now that, he thought, is a real meal. He dropped the rabbit and set off in chase of the deer. But the deer was too quick, and the chase was too long. So, puffing a bit, the lion came back to eat the rabbit. But the rabbit was nowhere to be seen.

"Serves me right," said the lion, "I should have been satisfied with what I had instead of running after bigger prey."

The moral that Aesop drew: "Be satisfied with what you have."

The Lark and the Farmer

No wonder parents have wanted to read the fable "The Lark and the Farmer" to their children. It tells a story with the moral of "do it yourself."

The young larks heard a farmer telling his son that he would have to hire some help to cut the corn. The mother lark told the young larks not to pay any attention to that kind of talk. The very next day, however, the farmer came to the field again and saw that the corn was beginning to fall to the ground.

"No time to lose," he told his son. "Go hire some men. We will start reaping the corn at once."

The mother lark heard that the farmer intended to start reap-ing the corn himself; she told the family to begin preparations for leaving. "For, once a man intends to do something himself, then he really means business. We must be off at once before it is too late." Aesop's conclusion: "Don't rely on others. If you want something done, do it yourself."

The Horse and the Donkey

There was once a fine thoroughbred black horse who lived in the same stable as a humble gray donkey. On market days, the donkey was weighed down with bags and bundles of food and wood and had to carry this load all the way home. The horse, meanwhile, had nothing else to carry but the farmer. The donkey patiently carried his load every week until one day he wasn't feeling too well and he asked the horse to give him some help in carrying the load.

"You've got to be joking," said the horse. "It would be beneath my dignity to assist you. My job is to carry men on my back, not goods and chattels. So get on with you and keep out of my way."

The donkey kept going until at last his legs gave way and he collapsed on the ground. The farmer saw that the donkey was in-deed ill and couldn't go any further. He took the heavy load from the donkey's back and put it onto the horse. Then he lifted the donkey and laid him across the horse's back. The horse never left off moaning all the way home. But the donkey told him that if he'd only helped when the donkey had asked him to, he wouldn't have the load to carry later.

Aesop's conclusion: "Always help others because you may need their help one day."

The Frog and the Ox

Some frogs were playing by a pool when an ox came down and accidentally trod on one of them, crushing him to death. The other frogs ran to his mother to report the casualty.

"Your son is dead," they told the mother frog. "He was trampled on by the biggest creature we've ever seen."

The mother frog cried for her lost son. Then she turned to the other frogs and asked if the animal was really as big as they said. She puffed herself out as big as she possibly could. "Was he as big as this?" she asked.

"Oh, much bigger," they said. The mother frog puffed herself out much more. "Was it as big as this then?" she asked. "Yes! Yes! Much bigger. You could never puff yourself up as big as that creature," the frogs told her. The mother was annoyed that any creature should be bigger than she.

"I'm the biggest," she said. "I'm as big as that creature," she gasped with one last gigantic puff. And with that last gasp, there was a loud bang and the mother frog burst and collapsed flat on the ground.

Aesop's conclusion: "Don't try to be bigger than you really are. "

The Mouse and the Bull

A mouse once bit a bull's tail, which made the bull so cross he jumped up and chased the mouse across the fields and into the yard. The mouse was too quick for the bull and slipped into a hole in the wall. The bull put down his head and charged the wall furiously time and again, bruising his head and chipping his horns. But the mouse stayed inside the wall.

At last the bull gave up and sank exhausted to the ground. He roared and fumed because he couldn't get at the mouse. The bull was just dozing off when a little voice cried from inside, "Big people don't always win; sometimes we little people come off best."

Aesop's conclusion: "The strong don't win every battle." This fable by Aesop has brought joy and consolation to the hearts of millions of children and adults who must have identified with the mouse when the mouse said, "Sometimes we little people come off best."

The Frog and the Mask

There was once an actor who had a large house with a large garden, and in the garden was a beautiful pond full of water lilies. And in the pond lived a family of frogs.

One day the smallest frog decided he wanted to see what was outside the pond and he hopped towards the house. He saw an open door and went inside. There was no one about, so he hopped into every room. He hopped on to the dressing table and busied himself with the various pots of cream and grease paint that he found there. With his face covered in cream and paint, he began hopping about in the cupboard when he suddenly stopped short.

In front of him was a face, a real face, lying on its own without a body. The little frog was frightened, but he was determined to get to know the face, so he held out his hand and touched the face. Then he laughed. It wasn't a real face, only a mask. "You may be a beautiful face," said the frog, "but I've got brains and you haven't."

The conclusion that Aesop drew: a beautiful face without brains is an empty face.

The Rabbits and the Frogs

"The rabbits were very unhappy," said Aesop the slave in this fable written more than five hundred years before the time of Christ, the Rabbits were very unhappy; they were badly treated by everyone. Men, dogs, eagles, and crows were their enemies, and they did not have the strength to fight back.

Sooner than be persecuted any longer, they decided to escape their misery and kill themselves. In a large group, they made their way to a lake, intending to drown themselves. By the side of the lake sat a family of frogs. When the frogs heard the rabbits coming, they leapt into the water panic-stricken and hid.

An old rabbit who had been leading the group stopped and said, "Here are some creatures who think we are bigger and stronger than they are. Take heart; we are not the most timid of beasts. Let us try to be as brave and strong as the water creatures think we are."

Aesop's moral: There is always someone worse off than you.

The Ant and the Grasshopper

An ant had been working night and day all summer, gathering a store of grain for the winter. Grain by grain he had carried it from the field and stored it away in a hole in a bank. Once he had collected it all, he set to work to dry it so that it would keep better.

A grasshopper was hopping by, cold and hungry. He saw the ant drying the grain and begged for a few grains. "I can't find any food anywhere," he cried. "And I'm starving; please spare me some of yours."

"But I've worked hard all summer to save this," said the ant. "I never stopped for one moment."

"Neither did I," said the grasshopper. "I never stopped singing all summer, and I was far too busy to collect food."

"In that case," said the ant, "you can dance all winter to keep warm. You won't get a grain of food from me."

Aesop's conclusion: Always save in the good times for the bad times to come.

The Frogs and the Well

Aesop's fables are appreciated by parents because their simple and charming folklore make it extremely easy to get over common sense to children. Consider this story of the Frogs and the Well:

The summer had been very hot and the marshes and rivers were drying up fast; animals of the forest were on the move to find water to drink. Two frogs had left their marsh in an effort to find another damp place. They were tired and thirsty when they found an old well. One of the frogs stood at the edge of the well and looked down.

"Come on," he said to his companion, "there's some cool water at the bottom. This seems to be a nice place to settle."

The other frog thought for a moment. "Just a minute, suppose this well dries up too? How will we be able to get out of it?"

"We would have a problem," agreed the first frog, and they both left the well and continued their search for water.

Concludes Aesop: "Think twice before making a quick decision. You can imagine how simple it would be for a parent to use this simple fable to tell their children about the dangers of making quick decisions."

The Cat and the Parrot

A cat was fast asleep on the rug in front of the fire when she was wakened by the sound of loud shrieks and squawks. Thinking that someone was being killed, she jumped to her feet and went to investigate. Her back arched and her hairs stood on end at what she saw. It was a highly colored parrot flying about the house, flapping its wings, crying with delight at being free. At last it landed on the mantlepiece.

"Who are you and what are you doing making such a terrible noise? You woke me up from my sleep."

The parrot screeched with laughter. "I can make as much noise as I like."

The cat glared at the bird. "If I were you, I'd keep quiet. I was born in this house, and those who live here are always telling me to be quiet. If I make a noise, they put me out in the yard."

"That's your problem. The master brought me here for my voice, so I'm going to let him hear it all day long," said the parrot, who then continued to shriek at the top of his voice.

Aesop's conclusion: Each one of us has a different role in life.

The Dog in the Manger
and
The Gnat and the Bull

A dog was accidentally shut in a manger with some horses.

He lay down on the hay and snarled at any horse that tried to feed from it.

"Don't be so selfish," said the horses. "If you don't want to eat the hay yourself, then let others who do want it have some."

Let others have what you don't want, concludes Aesop. The world remembers that story as "The Dog in the Manger."

Here is another fable you will enjoy:

A bull was grazing in a field when a gnat, which had been buzzing round his head for some time, finally settled on one of his horns.

"I do hope I'm not disturbing you," said the gnat. "I'm just having a little rest."

"Not at all," said the bull. "To tell you the truth, I didn't even know you were there until you spoke."

Aesop's conclusion: You are not always as important as you think. These fables of Aesop contain so much of the wisdom of the ages that we can all learn from them.

The Ant and the Dove

I think you would like to hear the fable by Aesop about the Ant and the Dove. Undoubtedly, you heard it as a child. This will give you a chance to recapture those days and find out once again where our common saying "one good turn deserves another" comes from.

One day an ant was drowsing, says Aesop, by the side of a pool and accidentally fell into the water. A dove cooing on a branch of a nearby tree, looked down, and saw that the ant couldn't swim, so she pecked off a leaf from the tree and tossed it into the pool. It landed near the ant who leapt onto it and floated on the water until a breeze came up and blew the leaf onto dry land. Now the ant was able to crawl off and shake himself dry. While he was doing this, he saw a bird-catcher creeping up to the dove. "Oh, no," said the ant, "I must help my savior."

So he jumped onto the man's leg and bit it hard. The man dropped the net in order to scratch the bite, and by the time he had picked up the net again, the dove had flown to safety.

Aesop's conclusion: "One good turn deserves another."

The Crow and the Pitcher

Have you wondered where we get the saying "Necessity is the mother of invention?" Listen to this fable by Aesop: It had been a very hot, dry summer. A very thirsty crow had spent the whole day searching for something to drink.

"I shall die of thirst," he said to himself, "unless I find a drop to drink!" Suddenly he saw a jug in the garden, under a tree. There was some water in it, the crow could see it, and could smell it, but it was at the bottom of the jug. No matter how he stretched his beak, he couldn't reach the water. Then he tried to break the top of the jug off with his beak. This failed. Now he tried to knock it over. No, that wouldn't do it. He flew at the jug, flapping his wings. But the jug stayed upright.

He flew to a tree and thought of a plan. "I must find some stones," he told himself and hopped to the ground. He fetched a pile of pebbles and began to drop them into the jug. With each stone, the water rose in the jug until, with the last stone, the water reached the brim and the clever crow was able to quench his thirst.

Aesop's moral: Necessity is the mother of invention.

The Fox and the Sick Lion

Aesop's Fable: "The Fox and the Sick Lion" has a moral for us. The lion was ill and all day long he lay in his lair moaning and groaning and sighing deeply whenever he heard anyone near.

The animals felt sorry for him because he was their king, and they knew he would be angry if no one visited him. So they agreed to visit him in small groups, thinking that if the lion was ill, he would be too weak to eat them. But they were wrong because once they were inside the lair, the lion pounced on them and ate them up.

It was only the fox who would never go into the lion's den. When the lion called out to him and asked him why he wouldn't come in to visit, the fox replied: "I see all the footprints in the sand point into your cave. But I don't see any footprints coming out. So I think I'll give visiting you a miss," and saying this, the fox ran quickly from the lion's den.

The moral drawn by Aesop: "Think for yourself and don't follow the crowd."

The Dog and the Donkey

As a child, you—as millions of other children throughout the centuries—enjoyed *Aesop's Fables*. As we get older, we still enjoy the fables and are in a better position to appreciate the little moral that Aesop adds to each fable.

"A little dog and a donkey lived with a farmer who looked af-ter them well," Aesop begins one of his fables. The donkey did all the work and the dog did none. All the dog did was play games with a bouncy ball, run around the fields, and at night made his bed in the best chair in the parlor while his master stroked him and told him he was a good little dog.

One night the donkey broke out of his stable and copied all the little dog's antics... even leaping onto the farmer's best chair and smashing it.

"Get out, you stupid beast," yelled the farmer, raising his fist.

"Go back to the stable. You'll get no food tonight."

Aesop drew this moral: "Be content with your lot and don't envy others."

The Dog and the Shadow

One of the reasons why the fables by the slave Aesop have been so enjoyed by children and their parents for the past thousand years is that they seem so true to the lives of each of us.

Consider Aesop's fable entitled "The Dog and the Shadow:" It happened that a Dog had gotten a piece of meat and was carrying it home in his mouth to eat it in peace. Now on his way home, he had to cross a plank lying across a running brook. As he crossed, he looked down and saw his own shadow reflected in the water beneath. Thinking it was another dog with another piece of meat, he made up his mind to have that also. So he made a snap at the shadow in the water, but as he opened his mouth, the piece of meat fell out, dropped into the water, and was never seen more.

Aesop's moral: "Beware lest you lose the substance by grasping at the shadow."

The Cock and the Pearl

What is so appealing about *Aesop's Fables*? For more than two thousand years, children and adults have been reading *Ae-sop's Fables*.

These stories from the mouths of animals and their moral conclusions have been a part of the folk literature of Europe, the Middle East, and the Orient. The stories are simple, wise, and their conclusions are in the form of a moral punch line.

Try this one, "The Cock and the Pearl":

A Cock was once strutting up and down the farmyard among the hens when he espied something shining amid the straw. "Ho! Ho!" quote he, "that's for me," and he soon rooted it out from be-neath the straw. What did it turn out to be but a pearl that by some chance had been lost in the yard?

"You may be a treasure," quote master Cock, "to men who prize you, but for me I would rather have a single-barleycorn than a peck of pearls."

Aesop's moral: "Precious things are for those who can prize them."

The Wolf and the Lamb

Once upon a time, a Wolf was lapping at a spring on a hillside, when, looking up, what should he see but a Lamb just be-ginning to drink a little lower down. *There's my supper*, thought he, *if only I can find some excuse to seize it*. Then he called out to the Lamb, "How dare you muddy the water from which I am drinking?"

"Nay, master, nay," said Lambikin: "if the water be muddy up there, I cannot be the cause of it, for it runs down from you to me."

"Well, then," said the Wolf, "Why did you call me bad names this time last year?"

"That cannot be," said the Lamb: "I am only six months old." "I don't care," snarled the Wolf, "if it was not you, it was your father" and with that, he rushed upon the poor little Lamb and—ate her all up. But before she died, she gasped out—"Any excuse will serve a tyrant."

The Fox and the Grapes

Have you ever wondered where we got the phrase "sour grapes"? Here's the story by Aesop the slave, five hundred years before the time of Christ: One hot summer's day, a Fox was strolling through an orchard till he came to a bunch of grapes just ripening on a vine, which had been trained over a lofty branch. "Just the thing to quench my thirst," quote he. Drawing back a few paces, he took a run and a jump and just missed the bunch. Turning round again with a One, Two, Three, he jumped up, but with no greater success. Again and again he tried after the tempting morsel of the bunch of grapes, but at last he had to give it up, and walked away with his nose in the air, saying: "I am sure they are sour."

Aesop's conclusion was: "It is easy to despise what you cannot get."

And that is where we get our meaningful phrase: "Sour Grapes."

Do Not Trust Flatterers

Do you remember the fable of the fox and the crow? A fox once saw a crow high up in a tree with a wonderful piece of cheese in its beak. "That's for me, as I am a fox," slyly said Master Renard, and he walked up to the foot of the tree. "Good-day, good-day, Mistress Crow," he cried. "How well you are looking today; oh, how glossy your feathers; how bright your eye. I feel sure your voice must surpass that of the other birds, just as your figure does; let me hear but one song from you, that I may greet you as Queen of Birds."

The crow was thus overcome by her own worth; she lifted up her head and began to caw her best, but the moment she opened her mouth, her treasure, the piece of cheese, fell to the ground, only to be snapped up by Master Fox. Mistress Crow continued to crow.

"That will do, that will do," said Master Fox. "That was all I wanted. In exchange for your treasure, the cheese, I will give you a piece of advice for the future: 'Do not trust flatterers.'"

The Lion and the Mouse

Once when a Lion was asleep, a little Mouse began running up and down on him; this soon wakened the Lion, who placed his huge paw upon him and opened his big jaws to swallow him. "Pardon, O King," cried the little Mouse, "forgive me this time, I shall never forget it: who knows but what I may be able to do you a turn some of these days?"

The Lion was so tickled at the idea of the Mouse being able to help him, that he lifted up his paw and let him go. Some time after the Lion was caught in a trap, and the hunters, who desired to carry him alive to the king, tied him to a tree while they went in search of a wagon to carry him on.

Just then the little Mouse happened to pass by, and seeing the sad plight in which the Lion was, he went up to him and soon gnawed away the ropes that bound the King of Beasts.

"Was I not right?" asked the little Mouse.

Aesop's moral: *"Little friends may prove great friends."*

The Town Mouse and the Country Mouse

Now you must know that a Town Mouse once upon a time went on a visit to his cousin in the country, writes Aesop. The Town Mouse rather turned up his nose at simple country life and invited his cousin to his town house. No sooner said than done: the two mice set off for the town and arrived at the Town Mouse's residence late at night.

"You will want some refreshment after our long journey," said the polite Town Mouse, and he took his friend into the grand dining room. There they found the remains of a fine feast, and soon the two mice were eating up jellies and cakes and all that was nice.

Suddenly they heard growling and barking. "What is that?" asked the Country Mouse.

"It is only the dogs of the house," answered the other.

"Only!" said the Country Mouse. "I do not like that music at my dinner." Just at that moment, the door flew open, in came two bull dogs, and the two mice had to scamper down and run off.

"Good-bye, Cousin," said the Country Mouse.

"What! Going so soon?" asked the other.

"Yes," he replied: "Better beans and bacon in peace than cakes and ale in fear."

The Wolf and the Crane

A Wolf had been gorging on an animal that he had killed, when suddenly a small bone in the meat stuck in his throat and he could not swallow it. He soon felt terrible pain in his throat, and he ran up and down groaning and seeking for something to relieve his pain. He tried to induce everyone whom he met to remove the bone. "I would give anything," he said, "if you would take it out."

At last the Crane agreed to try; it told the Wolf to lie on his side and open his jaws as wide as he could. Then the Crane put its long neck down the Wolf's throat, and with its beak loosened the bone, till at last it got it out.

"Will you kindly give me the reward you promised?" asked the Crane.

The Wolf grinned, showed his teeth, and said: "Be content. You have put your head inside a Wolf's mouth and taken it out again in safety; that ought to be reward enough for you."

Aesop's Moral: "Gratitude and greed go not together."

The Lion's Share

Aesop's fables were written five hundred years before the time of Christ, and we can't expect its conclusions to be Christian, but there is a good deal of natural wisdom in Aesop's conclusion to this Fable: "The Lion's Share":

The Lion went once a-hunting along with the Fox, the Jackal, and the Wolf. They hunted and they hunted till at last they surprised a Stag, and they soon took its life. Then came the question of how the spoil should be divided. "Quarter me this Stag," roared the Lion, so the other animals skinned it and cut it into four parts. Then the Lion took his stand in front of the carcass and pronounced judgment: "The first quarter is for me in my capacity as King of Beasts; the second is mine as arbiter, another share comes to me for my part in the chase; and as for the fourth quarter, well, as for that, I should like to see which of you will dare lay a paw upon it."

"Humph," grumbled the Fox, as he walked away with his tail between his legs; but he spoke in a low growl—"You may share the labours of the great, but you will not share the spoil."

The Man and the Serpent

A *Countryman's* son by accident trod upon a Serpent's tail, which turned and bit him so that he died. The father in a rage got his axe, and pursuing the Serpent, cut off part of its tail. So the Ser-pent in revenge began stinging several of the Farmer's cattle and caused him severe loss.

Well, the Farmer thought it best to make it up with the Ser-pent, brought food and honey to the mouth of its lair, and said to it:

"Let's forget and forgive; perhaps you were right to punish my son, and take vengeance on my cattle, but surely I was right in trying to revenge him; now that we are both satisfied, why should not we be friends again?"

"No, no," said the Serpent, "take away your gifts; you can never forget the death of your son, nor I the loss of my tail."

Aesop's moral: "Injuries may be forgiven, but not forgotten." Aesop's conclusion with animals is quite different from Christ's conclusion with human beings, that we should forgive and forget.

Peanuts Theology
Peanuts: Introduction

The newspaper cartoon Peanuts has had an amazing impact on the world. One hundred million readers of a thousand newspapers in a hundred countries read *Peanuts*. The exploits of Charlie Brown, Lucy Van Pelt, Linus, Sally, Peppermint Patty, Schroeder, Pig-Pen, and the whole gang of li'l folk, especially the dog Snoopy, are well known around the globe. For more than a third of a century, these creations of the deceased Charlie Schulz have dominated the world of cartoons and its by-products.

For instance, on one evening in New York City, Charlie Brown simultaneously played before a sell-out crowd for the stage show, a sell-out audience for the feature at the Radio City Music Hall, and a repeat network television special seen by 55 million Americans. No performer in the history of cartoons or show business has had such a record. More than that, just as the Bible is the all-time best seller, *Peanuts*, in one way a derivative of the Bible, is second in line for the all-time best-seller claim.

In a series of media presentations, we shall try to illustrate how *Peanuts and its message of the Bible Good News has de-served its popularity.*

Charles M. Schulz

The Bible is the world's all-time, overall, best seller. Peanuts is the world's all-time cartoon best seller.

There is a close relationship between the Bible and Peanuts.

Charles Schulz, the creator of Peanuts, was not only a product of the Divinity School of the University of Chicago, but he was a lay Bible teacher who flatly stated: "I preach in these cartoons, and I reserve the same rights to say what I want to say as the minister in the pulpit."

It all began when a child by the name of Charles Monroe Schulz skipped two grades in elementary school. Suddenly he was the youngest, smallest boy in his class. Always last to be chosen for teams, never asked to birthday parties, during lunch periods usually left to eat his peanut butter sandwiches in solitude, and after school left alone to be with his dog and his reams of drawing.

The rest is history. The incredible story of the internationalization of that little cast of characters known as the Peanuts gang. Over the past thirty-six years, it has enlivened the newspapers and stages and sales counters of the world with storms of laughter and unforgettable insights into the wry, richly human, completely Christian, and thoroughly hilarious imagination of the deceased Charles M. Schulz.

Its Bible base deserves retelling.

The Gospel According to Peanuts

Charlie Brown, Lucy Van Pelt, Linus, Sally, Peppermint Patty, Schroeder, Pig-Pen, and the whole retinue of the *Peanuts* tiny theatre speak in such biblical terms that a certain professor decided to write a book entitled *The Gospel According to Peanuts*. Within a short time, it sold more than 2 million copies.

More importantly, Dr. Robert Short found that American college youth know practically nothing about Christianity. "I offer as one rather typical example of what I mean by our (spiritual) 'flabbiness'—and as

119

God is my witness, I do not lie: One senior at a very fashionable and well-known New England girls' college asked me: 'Would you mind going over that "sin" business again?

Our teachers here in the Religion Department have never mentioned it." I cried and laughed most of the rest of the evening," concluded Dr. Short.

Friends, you have heard a good deal about the evils of our modern media in the reports on pornography. I suggest that you look at the other side of the American media coin and consider what's in *The Gospel According to Peanuts*.

Peanuts and Street Preaching

Charles Schulz, the creator of Peanuts, that famous comic strip, has had experience in street preaching. Here is his account:

In our St. Paul, Minnesota, Bible class, we young people used to feel that we should make some sort of public stand for Christ, so we commenced holding outdoor testimony meetings at the Union Gospel Mission downtown. It was rather difficult for me, yet I felt driven to stand up at these meetings and say something. So, with the streetcars going by, I stepped out on the sidewalk and managed some way to make my statement for the Lord.

By the time we held our third such meeting, I had been elected president of the group, and it was my responsibility to give the main sermon. So I found myself that night standing on the side-walk preaching, without having any real ability for this sort of thing. Right in the middle of my sermon, I happened to glance over to my left, and there were three of my golfing buddies, staring at me in complete surprise. They did not even know that I attended church. But we survived this, too, and it was good for us. I think all Christians should have to go out and do some preaching like that."

And I believe that Charles Schulz continues that heroic street preaching in his worldwide newspaper cartoon called Peanuts.

The Theology of Peanuts

Basic themes of the internationally famous newspaper comic strip *Peanuts* are the inadequacy of human nature as seen in Char-lie Brown and the redemptive power of love as seen in the dog Snoopy. These basic themes are Christian doctrine. Charles Schulz, the creator of Peanuts, put it this way in a commencement address:

No matter what I consider to say [stated Charles Schulz), I come back to a passage in the New Testament that contains a truth in which I firmly believe. In the last chapter of the Gospel of John... we find Peter and his friends returning at dawn from fishing. A figure is standing on shore by a small charcoal fire. They gather round this fire, none daring to speak, when though they know it is Jesus who has been waiting for them, Jesus turns to Peter, and asks, "Simon, son of John, do you love me more than these?" "Yes, Lord; you know that I love you."

When the excitement of these days passes away, [concludes Charles Schulz), and when some of the visions begin to grow a little dim, when it becomes impossible to put into words the prayer you want to speak, then we must be able to lift our heads up, and say with all faith as Peter did, "Lord, you know that I love you."

Charlie Brown I

"I feel terrible, I hate myself," says Charlie Brown. "I'd like to be able to feel that I'm needed.... I get tired of always being alone.... Why does everybody hate me?" These are regular refrains of Charlie Brown in the world-famous comic strip *Peanuts*. But strangely enough, no one hates Charlie Brown and from the assent of his 100 million readers, it seems he is very much loved.

What is there about Charlie Brown that makes him so popular with the newspaper readers of the world? The answer is that everyone can identify with him. Just like Charlie, all of us wish to love and be loved, to win and be recognized. Charlie has a globelike head that the other kids enjoy ridiculing; he may be a zero, a walking cipher, and a "no one" as he says, but he also is an "everyone," a modern "everyman." Charlie Brown's perfectly round head is a built-in halo with the face of all mankind in it.

We all understand Charlie when he feels with St. Paul: "The good that I want to do, I fail to do." All of us are aware, as was St. Paul, of the two laws that fight within us: "The law of the spirit and the law of the flesh... that which I would do, I do not; that which I would not do, I do."

And who will save us from this divine dilemma? The creator of Charlie Brown, just as own Creator, knows: our personal Savior is our Lord Jesus Christ.

Charlie Brown II

Charlie Brown is the number one Peanut. We must understand Charlie Brown if we are to understand what this world-famous comic strip *Peanuts* is all about. Charlie Brown is a good guy who is a born loser. He does his best to win. It doesn't. matter whether it is winning a friend or a game or one of his struggles with his uncooperative kites; he just wants to win—anything. But he is constantly losing. Take his yearly spring ritual of trying to fly his kite. Some tree inevitably devours his kite while the kites of other children sail majestically in a clear sky. Or take his yearly fall ritual of trying to kick the football, which Lucy Van Pelt solemnly promises she will hold for him, only to pull it back at the last moment so that Charlie Brown ends up on his backside.

Charlie places his trust in human nature, and humanity betrays him. His team lost the last game by 143 to 0! At five cents a session with his lady psychiatrist, Lucy, he has run up a bill of $143, which he will never be able to pay! He is wishy-washy. He doesn't get around to doing his homework. Charlie Brown is a four-star loser. But what makes him a winner is the Christian environment in which his comic strip is encased. The troubles of this world are not to be compared with the glories of the next. Charlie Brown is the underdog, but his public feel that they are too. They identify with him, and they are all for him.

Charlie Brown's Father

"I have treated Charlie Brown's father in a fair amount of detail," says the cartoonist Charles Schulz, "because I have let it be known that he is very receptive to his son's impromptu visits to the barber shop. Most of this is autobiographical, for my dad always greeted me cordially when I would drop in at his barbershop, and I used to go there and sit and read the newspapers and magazines until he closed his shop in the evening."

Here is how Charles Schulz translates this relationship with his father into Charlie Brown's life in the *Peanuts* cartoon: In the first frame of the comic strip, we see Charlie Brown outside his father's barber shop, and he is saying: "My dad likes to have me come down to the barber shop, and wait for him."

The second frame expands that thesis: "No matter how busy he is, even if the shop is full of customers, he always stops to say 'Hi' to me.... I sit there on the bench until six o'clock when he's through, and then we ride home together." The final frame concludes with a Charlie Brown classic: "It really doesn't take much to make a dad happy...."

Charlie Brown: "I need all the friends I can get."

When Charlie Brown of *Peanuts* fame said "I need all the friends I can get," he was speaking for all of us.

And when his chief antagonist, Lucy Van Pelt, demanded "Define friend," Charlie gave us all some good ideas:

A friend is someone you can sock on the arm.

A friend is someone who will take the side with the sun in his eyes.

A friend is someone who's willing to watch the TV program you want to watch.

A friend is someone who likes you even when the other guys are around.

A friend is someone who accepts you for what you are.

A friend is someone who is not jealous if you have other friends.

A friend is someone who will hold a place in line for you.

A friend is someone who sticks up for you when you're not there.

Friends, friendship in action, is Christianity in action.

"Do unto others as you would have done unto you," says our Lord, and you will be a true friend.

You're In Love, Charlie Brown

The tender love story of Charlie Brown for the pretty little red-haired girl hasn't been written yet because it really hasn't happened yet.

Charlie is in love. We know that. But Charlie, wishy-washy as he is, cannot bring himself to tell that pretty little red-haired girl that he is very interested in her. He worships her from afar.

When the little red-haired girl unknowingly dropped her pencil and Charlie retrieved it and found teeth marks all over it, allowing him to conclude that "she's human," he all but fainted with joy. (But he still could not give her the valentine that he had prepared especially for her.)

Once when his teacher called upon Charlie to give his report, he became so flustered that instead of reading his report, he mistakenly read a secret love note stating: "Dear little red-haired girl how—I have longed to meet you!" And the class roared with laughter. Poor Charlie Brown.

But somehow or other, Charlie did receive a wonderful note that read: "I like you, Charlie Brown. Signed, Little Red Haired Girl." Charlie went into a rapturous delirium. The reading world mourns the loss of the completion of that tender love story, for it knows that if Charles Schulz were writing the script, it would be of classical beauty and genius proportions.

Paternal Hero Worship

Paternal hero worship is epidemic among the li'l ones in *Peanuts*.

Consider this scene: "My dad is taller than your dad," says Violet to Charlie Brown as they walk along. "My dad has broader shoulders than your dad and..." Violet continues, "my dad is better looking than your dad."

Charlie Brown becomes somewhat indignant and raises his voice: "Your dad!! You're always talking about your dad!! Maybe my dad isn't perfect, but I like him anyway!! He's my dad and I like him!!"

"You're screaming, Charlie Brown," admonishes Violet.

"I'm sorry... I didn't mean to scream," says Charlie, "I was only trying to say that I like my dad for what he is... he's my dad and I like him."

"That's very commendable, Charlie Brown," concludes Vio-let, "you are to be congratulated on your loyalty."

"Thank you," says a subdued Charlie.

But Violet persists: "However, my dad..."

And Charlie ends the strip by exclaiming: "Oh, good grief!" And what a relief it is for parents to know that their children are exposed to such paternal hero worship.

Psychiatric Help, Five Cents

Here is some psychiatric help for you. From the funny paper cartoon *Peanuts*. Charlie Brown comes up to Lucy who is behind her stand, over which you see the sign "Psychiatric Help Five Cents."

Says Charlie Brown: "What do you do when the world runs by you?"

"What do you do when nobody likes you?

"What do you think happens when you feel lost and alone?"

"Come on, Charlie," says Lucy, and she takes him to the high hill. "Charlie, see this world? See all the world around you? You don't know of any other world?"

"No."

"You were born in this world?"

"Ya."

"There is no other world in which you can live? Well, *Live In It.*"

Charlie is knocked off of his chair and lies flat on his back, and Lucy comes up and says, "Five cents, please." Lucy has given good psychiatric advice to Charlie Brown and all of us—let's get off our backs—stand up, face the world, and with God's help, "live in it."

Lucy Van Pelt

If Charlie Brown is the incarnation of the good, Lucy Van Pelt is the incarnation of the evil in the comic strip Peanuts. She is the one who regularly calls Charlie "Blockhead." She promises she will hold the football for Charlie Brown, but year after year she betrays him and laughs when he falls on his backside.

Lucy ridicules Charlie, "ol' wishy washy," she calls him, for being too moral to throw a bean ball.

She discourages her younger brother, Linus, for "that terrible drawing. You have absolutely no talent," she says. She is confirmed in her cross-grained crabbiness and revels in the fact that just as she is crabby little girl, she will be a crabby old woman.

Lucy plans to exclude other little people from her party so they'll feel bad. When asked what the present generation can do about all the social problems that it has inherited, she states with clenched teeth and fist, "Stick the next generation."

Schulz has said of Lucy: "Perhaps if you scratched deeper, you'd find she's even worse than she seems." Lucy seems to be Schulz's living proof that there is such a condition as original sin.

The World's Most Famous Psychiatrist

I wish to discuss with you the world's most famous psychiatrist. The name? Not Sigmund Freud, but Lucy Van Pelt. Dr. Lucy has given psychiatric advice to more persons in the world than Sigmund Freud ever dreamed of. She dispenses her psychiatric prescriptions from the *Peanuts* cartoons in a thousand newspapers and in a hundred countries. Her psychiatry office is no more than what appears to be a child's lemonade stand with a sign above it advertising: "Psychiatric Help 5e." Here are some of her psychiatric gems:

To Charlie Brown who constantly feels that no one likes him, Lucy points out that "There is no other world in which you can live... well, live in it."

To little Sally who confides: "I'm afraid of kindergarten, I don't know why... I'm just afraid..." psychiatrist Lucy gives this analysis: "You're no different from anyone else... five cents please."

To little Frieda who maintains that she is hated by other little girls because they are jealous of her and her naturally curly hair, Dr. Lucy boldly enunciates: "Don't kid yourself, sister... 5¢ please."

It is consoling to know that the script writer for these psychiatric prescriptions for a world audience, though not a physician, is one who is dedicated to a God whose name is Love and whose mercy is above all of his works.

Linus Van Pelt

Linus's security blanket is an international conversation piece.

Here is how Linus explains his need for his security blanket to his psychiatrist, Lucy:

"I'm in sad shape," says Linus. "My life is full of fear and anxiety. The only thing that keeps me going is this blanket. I need help."

Here's how Charles Schulz, the creator of *Peanuts*, explains the blanket: "Linus's affection for his blanket is a symbol of the things we cling to. What I am getting at, of course, is the adult's inadequacy, here the inability to give up habits which really should be given up. Not that I am completely against the idea that we have to cling to something! For once you accept Jesus, it does not mean that all of your problems are automatically solved, or that you will never be lonesome again. How can you be happy all the time, if you are aware of the things that are going on around you? But some of our adult habits are ridiculous."

Lucy says to Linus: "There's something about that blanket that annoys me!"

And Linus archly replies: "Why not try looking upon it as a conversation piece?"

The Meditations of Linus: On Age

Linus Van Pelt of the *Peanuts* newspaper comic strip is noted not only for his security blanket but also for his frequent Bible quotations. It was appropriate for the creator of *Peanuts*, Charles Schulz, and the Hallmark Cards Company to publish a booklet entitled *The Meditations of Linus*. The first meditation is entitled "Old Age."

In the first frame of this meditation, Linus is shaking his fist at his older sister, Lucy, saying: "I can't hit you now because you're bigger than I am... but you just wait... in a few more years, I'll be bigger than you are!"

Lucy responds: "By then I'll be a lady and you can't hit a lady." And in an unladylike way, Lucy sticks out her tongue and utters; "Nyah, nyah, nyah!"

Linus realizes the truth of his older sister's retort and concludes despairingly: "I'm living in a stacked deck." Friends, in a sense, Linus is correct. We are living in a stacked deck. There are very definite social differences and responsibilities according to whether we are born male or female. Boys and girls, men and women are inherently different. The overwhelming majority of the human race are very pleased with these differences of the sexes, and thank God for them, saying: "Long live the difference!"

The Meditations of Linus: On Doctor

The medical profession comes off poorly in the internationally syndicated comic strip Peanuts. The doctors are represented by a psychiatrist by the name of Lucy. She dispenses here mental-health prescriptions from what appears to be a lemonade stand with a sign above it advertising: "Psychiatric Help 5¢."

On this particular day, the doctor is "in," and Lucy is telling her patient Linus who has his right thumb in his mouth and his security blanket in his left hand: "If you'd listen to me, you wouldn't need that thumb and blanket...."

Linus replies quite smartly: "Years from now when your kind has passed from the scene, thumbs and blankets will still be around!" That smart remark is more than Dr. Lucy can stand, and with that well-known right fist, she knocks Linus off the patient's stool with a big POW! From the floor, Linus: "Doctors always tell you to say what's on your mind, but they don't really mean it...."

This inconsistency of doctors is again highlighted by Lucy after she has given Charlie her best psychiatric encouragement to get away from home and go to summer camp. Charlie asks her: "How about you? Are you going to camp this summer?"

Dr. Lucy indignantly replies: "And leave my good home? Don't be ridiculous!!!"

The Meditations of Linus: On Philosophy

"I think it is possible to be too nice!" says Lucy. "By golly, nobody's gonna walk over me! If anybody's gonna do any walking, it's gonna be me!" Lucy continues with her philosophy of life by concluding: "There's only one way to survive these days.... You have to walk over them before they walk over you!" Friends: If you believe that children are born naturally good, listen to what the creator of the *Peanuts* comic strip has to say:

"The one observation on which the strip initially was based," states Schulz, "is something I recall from seventh grade, when to my horror I saw two girls after class go over to another girl and say: "We're going to have a party this week, but we're not going to invite you. Now this girl was just crushed by this statement! It would have crushed me, but I was just like Charlie Brown —I knew I didn't have a ghost of a chance being invited anyway... but this is one of the basic themes of Peanuts, which is the cruelty that exists among these children."

The basic solution is also very clear. Over and over again, the cartoon presents the theme: "To you is born this day... a Savior, who is Christ the Lord" (Luke 2:11).

The Meditations of Linus: On Distraction

This meditation of Linus is called "On Distraction"; it is re-ally on distraction and procrastination.

"I'm bringing my teacher a birthday card," says Linus to Charlie Brown. "Maybe it will take her mind off the fact that I didn't get my math done."

Says Charlie Brown: "How do you think of things like that?" Replies Linus: "I'm always interested in anything that will cloud the issue."

There are many scenes in the Peanuts comic strips that mirror Charles Schulz's conviction that children are born procrastinators. As victims of the need for immediate gratification, they cannot bring themselves to the discipline of the difficult, such as doing their homework, unless their parents strategize them into it.

This proclivity for procrastination, this ability to distract oneself from doing the necessary, is forcefully dramatized in a scene in which Charlie is sweating it out in the classroom, waiting for the bell to ring so he won't be called upon to give the report that he did not prepare. "Come on, you stupid bell," he says, "ring! Don't just hang there on the wall! Ring! Come on! Ring!" And finally the bell did ring. And Charlie was saved until the morrow.

Linus then says to him: "Now you can go home and finish your report, huh, Charlie Brown? Then you won't have to worry about it tomorrow."

Replies Charlie: "Who cares about tomorrow? C'mon, let's play ball." No wonder he is known as wishy-washy. He is too much like the rest of us.

The Meditations of Linus: On Brotherly Love

"You're the worst kind of a little brother a girl could have," said Lucy to Linus. "If I could have had my choice, you would have been the last one I would have chosen!" Linus regains his composure by hollering after her. "Thirty years from now, you'll love me." And then he philosophically concludes to himself: "Big Sisters always love their brothers thirty years later."

Linus and other little brothers should take consolation from the fact that big sisters are not as bad as they sometimes seem. (Even Lucy went to the psychiatrist and confessed: "I have a strange problem, so I've come to you for help. I consider my brother as being a complete blockhead... yet now that he's gone off to camp, I miss him... what's wrong with me?")

The clinching proof of Lucy's present love for her little brother was the time when Lucy was her usual crabby self and was complaining to Linus: "I don't get half the breaks other people do ... nothing ever goes right for me! And you talk about counting blessings! You talk about being thankful! What do I have to be thankful for!"

To which Linus softly replied: "Well, for one thing, you have a little brother who loves you." There was a pause. Lucy had no answer for that, and she broke down and started to cry.

Such is the theme and power of the Gospel according to Peanuts.

The Meditation of Linus: On Symbolism

In this meditation we contemplate Lucy rolling the portable TV set out of the living room into her own room, but in the process running down her younger brother Linus who was quietly reading a book. Linus comments: "There's something symbolic about being run over by a portable TV while reading a book." The obvious symbolism is that TV has greatly replaced reading in our culture.

The religious symbolism of Charles Schulz's cartoons is the subject of Dr. Robert Short's two volumes entitled *The Gospel According to Peanuts and The Parables of Peanuts*. Charlie Brown is seen as the innocent, suffering Jesus or the twentieth century Everyman wearing a T-shirt of thorns. Lucy Van Pelt is seen as a crabby symbol of original sin. Schroeder, the Beethoven worshiper, is seen as a worldly-wise victim of Idolatry, and Snoopy, the most beloved "hound of heaven," is seen as a little Christ who afflicts the comfortable and comforts the afflicted; the tree that yearly devours Charlie Brown's kites is seen as the tree of the cross.

Mr. Charles Schulz states: "All kinds of people in religious work have written to thank me for preaching in my own way through the strips. That is one of the things that keep me going."

The Meditations of Linus: On Flowers

In the booklet entitled *The Meditations of Linus*, published by Hallmark Cards, Incorporated, Charles Schulz calls, the second meditation "On Flowers."

In this meditation we first see Linus Van Pelt watching Char-lie Brown pluck a daisy. Then Charlie begins picking off each petal of the daisy while saying: "She loves me... she loves me not; she loves me, she loves me not; she —" and Linus interrupts Charlie by saying: "It is difficult for me to believe that a flower has the gift of prophecy!"

Friends, what are we to say about this charming and biblically simple scene of Charlie and Linus? It is typical of Charles Schulz, its creator.

Charles Schulz states: "As a comic-strip artist, I feel called upon to be uplifting and decent.. I cannot fail to be thrilled every time I read the things that Jesus said, and I am more and more convinced of the necessity of following him. What Jesus means to me is this: In him we are able to see God, and to understand his feelings toward us."

It is this cosmic perspective that Charles Schulz tries to get over in his cartoon *Peanuts*. And he does so in an extraordinarily successful manner.

The Meditations of Linus: On Character Development

The Meditations of Linus is a booklet published by Charles Schulz and the Hallmark Cards Company. The meditation on "Character Development" is particularly charming and challenging. Linus is without his security blanket in this sequence. But his insecurity is apparent nevertheless. "Look at all this stuff," says

Linus, "games, clothes, a bicycle, baseball equipment... a transistor radio, books, candy this is terrible! This is my worst Christmas yet!" Charlie Brown looks on in amazement as Linus continues his tirade: "How will I develop any character?" And he concludes in all but complete desperation: "I always get everything I want!"

And this is really a challenge for responsible parents. How can their children develop their characters when in an affluent society they seem to receive everything they want. The answer to that honest concern can be gathered from other *Peanuts* considerations: as our society becomes more and more complicated, it also becomes more and more demanding of children in their education to become "civilization adequate."

Thank God that we all have such clever, artistic, and whole-some examples as those provided by the *Peanuts* gang.

Snoopy and the Red Baron

Snoopy is the best known dog in the world. Even before the moon shot, *Peanuts* was being carried in newspapers in sixty foreign countries. But the adoption by the Apollo crew of Snoopy as their watchdog and the success of the moon shot assured the name "Snoopy" becoming a household name throughout the world.

But what is the meaning beyond entertainment of Snoopy being regularly portrayed as a World War I airplane fighter pilot battling it out with the Red Baron? Considering the biblical background and commitment of the cartoonist, Charles Schulz, it seems to many that the Red Baron represents the evil of the world: "Curse the Red Baron and his kind!" exclaims Snoopy after getting shot down innumerable times. "Curse the wickedness in this world! Curse the evil that causes all this unhappiness!"

Snoopy as his cartoonist creator seems to be involved in the triumphant battle with the forces of evil. Thinly veiled in Jesus Christ's triumphant paean as recorded by John: "In the world you will have trouble. But courage! The victory is mine; I have conquered the world" (John 16:23). The forces of light have already defeated the forces of evil. Snoopy and Schulz are committed to seeing that the good news leaks out.

Schroeder

Schroeder and Beethoven are buddies in the *Peanuts* cartoon.

The other members of the *Peanuts* gang are not as fixed to any one musical instrument as Schroeder is to the piano, but all of them have an appreciation for art and music and literature that is unique in comic book presentations. Children who are fans of *Peanuts* and internationally there are millions —are influenced to believe by Peanuts that music, art, and religion rather than child porno, violence, and sexual abuse, are the human way to live.

Take this delightful scenario: Lucy, Linus, and Charlie Brown are gazing up at the clouds one day. Linus says: "That cloud looks a little like the profile of Thomas Eakins, the famous painter and sculptor... and that group of clouds over there gives me the impression of the stoning of Stephen.... I can see the Apostle Paul standing there to one side."

Says Lucy: "Uh-huh, That's very good. What do you see in the clouds, Charlie Brown?"

Charlie responds: "Well, I was going to say I saw a ducky and horsie, but I changed my mind."

Friends: The Peanut kids love the good things. They love meadows with green grass, songs with a melody, culture, and the good life. This speaks well for them and their tomorrows and for our tomorrows as well.

Happiness is... Home!

(Psychiatrist Lucy Van Pelt advises Charlie Brown to go to summer camp. Charlie responds: "How about you? Are you going to camp this summer?" Dr. Lucy indignantly replies: "And leave my good home? Don't be ridiculous!!!")

***

The refreshing attitude of the home and the family being of the essence of happiness makes *Peanuts* joyous reading. Year after year

Charlie Brown goes off to summer camp, and he explains why: "My mom and dad think they're doing me a favor... they're happy because they think this will be a good experience for me.'

Ten minutes on the camp bus is all that it takes to make Charlie feel lonesome. "I feel like I'm being drafted," he declares. Linus says that he is his dad's "built-in friend." Linus's mother sneaks notes into his lunch box that read: "Study hard today. Your father and I are very proud of you and want you to get a good education."

Linus finds separation from the family so disquieting that he suffers from fears of desertion: "What if Mother and Dad move away while I'm gone, and don't tell me?" he moans.

Sally wants to be just like Mom: "All I want to do when I grow up is to get married and be a good wife and mother.... Why should I have to go to kindergarten?" (Peppermint Patty's father calls her "rare gem.")

(The parents of the *Peanuts* on their side always find time to go to PTA meetings, Christmas pageants, Little League baseball games, and Schroeder's piano recital. They take time with their children, instruct them lovingly, and have confidence that their children will learn the right thing to do. The kids reflect this confidence.)

To the Peanuts, Happiness is... Home!

Blanket-Hating Grandmothers

If anyone gets shortchanged in the Peanuts comic strip, it is grandmothers.

Rather than a tender, loving, candy-laden, grand-child-spoiling grandmother, we have a disciplinarian, blanket-hating grandmother. (The cartoonist, Charles Schulz, tells us that Linus's blanket is a symbol of "the things we cling to." And what about Linus's blanket-hating grandma?) According to Lucy, "She believes children should be taught self-denial; she believes in discipline; she believes in moral fibre." And Linus adds, "She believes in butting into other people's business." (Grandma can't stand that security blanket of Linus and uses brute force to get the blanket from him. Linus fights back with strategic plans, such as using as colored dish towel as a decoy.) He also brings out that grandma is not free from her own security blanket. Charles Schulz explains, "Not long ago I had Linus's blanket-hating grandmother come to his house for a visit. She tried to get him to give up his propensity for the blanket so he threw up to her the fact that she was drinking thirty-two cups of coffee a day!"

It is with no little charm and much condescension that Linus discusses his grandmother with his pal Charlie Brown: "Well, my blanket-hanging grandmother will be here Monday," says Linus.

"Can't you hide your blanket before she comes?" asks Charlie.

"No," responds Linus, "I've got to let her take it away from me. This will make her feel that she has accomplished something. She needs understanding."

Conclusion: Peanuts and the Children of the World

What impact has the phenomenally successful Peanuts had upon the children of the world? Jeffrey Loria of the New York School of Social Research concludes that the Peanuts kids "are probably the most stabilizing influence in America today...." With the psychic stability of children shaken to their foundations by the break-up of one out of two marriages, with educational demands being made of even infants ab utero with a cosmic atomic holocaust hanging over their heads, no wonder children need an in-house, on-call psychiatrist such as Lucy. Professor Carle C. Zimmerman of Harvard, with whom I have co-authored several books, maintains that our own society must be the psychiatrist for each of us. And that's what the Peanuts group has.

Consider not only Lucy on psychiatry, but Charlie on Love; Linus on the Bible; Snoopy on leisure-time activities. Politics, school, home, sports, religion, friendship... the whole of Western culture is viewed realistically and idealistically through the eyes of the Peanuts kids. Charles Schulz has given us, as theologian Dr. Robert L. Short had documented: *The Gospel According to Peanuts.*

We close with a classroom scene from *Peanuts*. The pupils are reciting: "I pledge allegiance to the flag of the United States of America and to the Republic for which it stands, one nation, under God, indivisible, with liberty and justice for all." There is a pause, and little Sally adds, "AMEN."

*Dr. Robert L. Short, The Gospel According to Peanuts, New York: Bantam Books, Inc. 1968.

www.ingramcontent.com/pod-product-compliance
Lightning Source LLC
Chambersburg PA
CBHW030920140626
46545CB00016B/2144